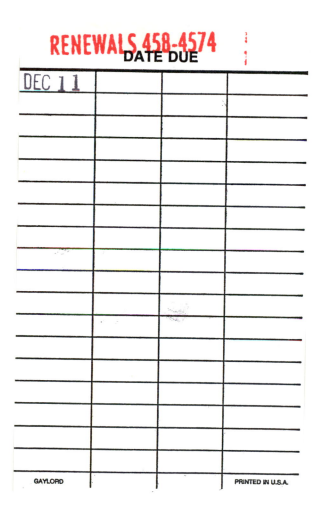

Strategic Planning
and
Performance Management

STRATEGIC PLANNING AND PERFORMANCE MANAGEMENT

DEVELOP AND MEASURE WINNING STRATEGY

◆

GRAHAM KENNY

ELSEVIER
BUTTERWORTH
HEINEMANN

AMSTERDAM BOSTON HEIDELBERG LONDON NEW YORK OXFORD
PARIS SAN DIEGO SAN FRANCISCO SINGAPORE SYDNEY TOKYO

Elsevier Butterworth-Heinemann
Linacre House, Jordan Hill, Oxford OX2 8DP
30 Corporate Drive, Burlington, MA 01803

First published in Australia as *Strategic Factors*, by President Press 2001
First published by Elsevier 2005

British Library Cataloguing in Publication Data
A catalogue record for this book is available from the British Library

Library of Congress Cataloguing in Publication Data
A catalogue record for this book is available from the Library of Congress

ISBN 0 7506 6383 9

For information on all Elsevier Butterworth-Heinemann publications
visit our website at http://www.books.elsevier.com

Printed and bound in Great Britain

Working together to grow
libraries in developing countries

www.elsevier.com | www.bookaid.org | www.sabre.org

ELSEVIER   BOOK AID
International   Sabre Foundation

To my mother and father, Doris and Coyne Kenny,
for their love and inspiration.

To my wife, Margaret, for her love and support.

To my children, Shaun and Joanne, for their love
and understanding.

CONTENTS

F O R E W O R D

Throughout a career providing advisory services to clients across several industries, I have seen the majority grappling with the best way to develop, implement and measure strategy and performance. In *Strategic Planning and Performance Management* Graham Kenny provides a refreshingly simple method for doing precisely that — which is what makes this a great book!

Through a distinguished consulting and academic career, Graham has observed many businesses taking varied approaches to strategy and has used that experience to develop a methodology and software system that can only be described as a breakthrough: it logically focuses on all the key stakeholders of an organization and develops objectives and a strategic plan that suits them. His company's approach also seeks to highlight a business' differentiators.

The key to a successful organization in today's increasingly competitive marketplace is the ability to differentiate your product or service to *all* your key stakeholders. The *Strategic Planning and Performance Management* methodology brilliantly focuses on an 'outside-in' approach to strategy and competitive advantage. Too many businesses focus on internal processes and an internal perception of competitive advantage in order to gauge the success of their strategy and operations. Graham's example (just one of many highly useful case studies) of a business that implemented a new computer system and then considered that it had automatically achieved a competitive advantage is particularly powerful, given the levels of investment in Information Technology in all industries and the true value brought to business through those systems.

Competitive advantage and differentiation can only be measured by an organization's key stakeholders, by what drives their choices; strategy and measures must be established around those needs.

The *Strategic Planning and Performance Management* methodology sets out first of all to identify the stakeholders and prioritise them. It then seeks to determine what the organization's strategic factors are, defining them as what is important to the key stakeholders. By setting targets around those strategic factors and putting in place a real-time, leading-indicator measurement system, the methodology provides business with the tools to gauge success and to identify early warning signs if things are off track.

If you are honest with yourself when looking at your own strategic plans, I am sure you will see significant inconsistencies between your objectives, aims, processes and targets; more than likely your plan mixes the lot. The package of the Strategic Factor System, including this book, the software and Graham's strategy workshops, will help focus the attention of your company or business unit on what is really critical and on how you can best go about achieving competitive advantage.

Strategic Planning and Performance Management is a significant step forward in strategic planning and performance measurement.

Peter Russell
Partner
KPMG

PREFACE

I remember writing the first few pages of this book and thinking: what now? Sure, I'd written papers, articles and manuals, but a book? That was a task of different proportions.

The first version of the book wasn't right — too much use of the passive voice and too academic. The second version of the book overcorrected and went to another extreme. The third version is the one you have here.

While rewriting delayed the book's progress, other events caused additional interruptions: the actual development of the methods and the patenting process.

Over the last several years the System — we call it the Strategic Factor System — has evolved and taken firm shape. While it has a history dating back to 1990, only in the last few years have certain key elements fallen into place. These necessitated restructuring and rewriting as well.

The patenting process also caused lengthy but important delays. Patenting is a detailed and tedious procedure not recommended for the free of spirit. But it was a very significant one for us. It forced us to distil the essence of our System into a precise description. (See Intellectual Property Rights.)

Of course, there were other delays, such as running a business, earning a living, raising a family and being involved in various community organizations. I was, for example, President of my Rotary Club for the standard period of one year during the writing and development of the book.

But these activities helped the book to mature. I refer particularly to the public seminars I run on strategic planning and key performance indicators, our company's consulting activities in these areas, and our development of software. All this work has constantly refined the ideas presented here.

We've learned a great deal from our clients: what works

and what doesn't, what they like and what they don't like, what they find useful and what they find extraneous. This feedback has helped us to continually refine, improve and simplify our System.

The development of software for strategic analysis, strategy development and performance measurement has also been a learning experience requiring discipline and rigor. It is a matter of breaking something into its smallest elements and writing code around the latter. The people in our company have produced leading-edge products that capture our System. (One such product assists users to develop a Focused Scorecard of key performance indicators for a business unit or organization, while another also links all scorecards in an organization together.)

Much work has indeed gone into our Strategic Factor System, and the beauty of the System is: *it works*!

The benefits to you from reading this book are potentially enormous. It will change your approach to strategic analysis, strategy formulation and performance measurement, forever. Guaranteed.

How can I be so confident? Because I've witnessed such change with my own eyes. I've seen the way the more than 4,000 people I've worked with have grasped our simple yet powerful System. I've seen the veil lift from their eyes as they came to understand strategic factors and how to employ them. I've seen how pleased they were to cast off their complicated and ineffective approaches and adopt simpler methods. I've seen the way the lights go on in people's eyes as they realize they've come upon a method that makes sense. I've heard their relief that finally someone has been able to link it all together in a logical way. I've received letters from people thanking me for introducing them to our System and for making their life easier.

I hope that through this book, you, too, will be able to effectively develop, measure and manage winning strategies. What is called for is a clear understanding of strategy and the foundations of effective strategy and performance measurement. In this book, we call these fundamental building blocks "strategic factors". The concept is new and has been developed over many years by assisting organizations to undertake analysis, write strategy, put this into a strategic plan and measure strategic success.

I also hope that through *Strategic Planning and Performance Management* I can help to eliminate much of the confusion that exists in managers' minds regarding how to formulate strategy and measure performance. Were each member of your planning or measurement team to adopt the framework outlined in this book, your organization or business unit would experience less confusion and produce better results.

If this book can empower you via these various ways, it will be a success.

Strategic Planning and Performance Management is intended for *all* employees, managers or not, in organizations of *all* types and sizes – *manufacturing* or *service, large* or *small*. It is intended for people in *non-profit* as well as *profit* organizations. It is aimed at people managing an *organization as a whole* or a *business unit* such as a product division or a support department like human resources. It is directed at people in both the *public* and *private sectors* who wish to develop and measure strategy that focuses energy in the right direction and leads to success.

I wanted to make this book practical, so I've structured each chapter for maximum clarity regarding the relevant basic concepts and amply demonstrated the concepts by examples. These examples are not simply passing references or throw-away anecdotes. They are, as much as the book allows, substantial cases of organizations that have developed strategy and key performance indicators.

Because the task of analyzing, developing and measuring strategy can become confusing and complicated, *Strategic Planning and Performance Management* is intended to make life easier — for you, your colleagues and fellow employees.

Please let us know how you succeed. We'd be delighted to hear from you.

Graham Kenny
Strategic Factors
PO Box 702

Mosman NSW 2088
Australia
Fax: (Sydney) 612 9969 2596
E-mail: gkenny@strategicfactors.com
Website: www.strategicfactors.com

ACKNOWLEDGMENTS

Although I am the sole author of this book, I am not the sole author of the System described in this book. Moreover, the writing of a book is by no means a single person project.

Margaret Kenny is the co-author of the Strategic Factor System. I'd like to thank her from the bottom of my heart. As business partner, fellow Company Director and wife, Margaret has worked with me over many years to develop the System. She leads the development of intellectual property by our company, bringing to it extensive experience in business and technology as an analyst, manager and lecturer. Margaret holds the degrees of Master of Commerce and Bachelor of Business.

I am grateful to Catherine Hammond for her editing of the manuscript. She has done a marvellous job in restructuring the material and providing the skills that have made the text much more interesting. Her experience, imagination and intelligence have been immeasurable assets.

I'd like to acknowledge the assistance of Penny McCann, who tirelessly typed and re-typed this manuscript over its lengthy journey, always cheerfully. Penny has also made constructive comments as to content and structure. For her patience and help, I thank her.

Thank you to John Porte for his contribution. His calm and intelligent input has helped refine the System.

Bob Aley, a management consultant, acted as sample reader. His clear-thinking contribution to the book's final structure, style and content has been significant and is gratefully acknowledged here.

Thank you also to Jo Rudd for her helpful comments and editorial assistance, as well as for compiling an excellent index, and to Simon Leong for type and cover design.

I'd like to acknowledge my clients and everyone who has

attended my public seminars over the last twelve years. They have all given me the opportunity to explore ideas, tools and techniques with them. I thank them for assisting me along the way.

Last but not least, I'd like to acknowledge some of the people I've worked with over the years. Although none of them have had any direct input in this book or the development of the Strategic Factor System, working with them helped to shape my ideas. I'd especially like to thank Professor Bob Hinings of the University of Alberta, Canada; Professor David Hickson, formerly at the University of Bradford Management Centre in the United Kingdom; Professor Alan Dunk of the University of Tasmania in Australia; Professor Dexter Dunphy from the University of Technology, Sydney; and Professor John Machin, formerly of the Durham University Business School in the United Kingdom. My work with these people has covered topics such as objective setting, performance measurement, power, inter-organizational relations, decision-making and strategy. To each of them I have an intellectual debt which I acknowledge here.

Let me finally acknowledge the work of Professor Michael Porter from the Harvard Business School. Since 1980, with his first book, *Competitive Strategy*, he has been the person to watch in the strategy field. His work, always practical and incisive, has inspired me and sustained my efforts throughout the writing of this book.

ABOUT THE AUTHOR

Graham Kenny heads the company, Strategic Factors, which specializes in strategic planning and performance measurement.

His firm assists organizations to undertake strategic analysis, write strategic plans and measure performance. It does this, in part, through a facilitation process ensuring that ownership of whatever is produced remains with clients. Strategic Factors has also been responsible for developing innovative software for planning, producing key performance indicators and monitoring performance. Its products are all based on the company's Strategic Factor System.

For the past twelve years, Graham has conducted public seminars on strategic planning and performance measurement. He has met a vast array of organizational situations and problems. Coming to grips with each of them has strengthened his knowledge.

In the private sector he has consulted on strategic planning and performance measurement to clients in software development, electrical equipment, importing, mineral refining, food processing and packaging, banking, communications, pharmaceuticals, information services, paper products, health services, manufacturing, property development and hospitality industries. In the public sector, again in strategic planning and performance measurement, Graham has assisted clients in information services, trustee services, lotteries, horse racing, tax, railways, higher education, the armed forces, government research, health, technical repairs, rural finance, agriculture, electricity supply, treasury and water resources.

Graham's academic qualifications include a Doctor of Philosophy in Management from the University of New South

Wales, Australia, as well as a Master's Degree in Management from Durham University in the United Kingdom, and a Bachelor of Engineering from the Queensland University of Technology, Australia. He has been Professor of Management at San Diego State University, U.S.A., the University of Alberta and the University of New Brunswick, Canada; Visiting Research Fellow at the University of Bradford Management Centre in the United Kingdom; Visiting Scholar at the University of North Florida, U.S.A.; Adjunct Professor of Management at Bond University, Australia; and Senior Lecturer in Management at the University of Technology, Sydney.

Graham has published numerous articles in management journals throughout the world, some of which have been reproduced in U.S. management textbooks and translated into other languages. Journals have included *Journal of Management Studies, Human Relations, Canadian Journal of Administrative Sciences, Journal of General Management, Asia Pacific Journal of Management, Evaluation Review* and *IEEE Transactions on Engineering Management*.

Graham's commercial experience has also been extensive. As General Manager, he has been responsible for turning a loss-making manufacturer of timber building products into a profitable operation. He has been Plant Manager in a concrete company, a Market Development Manager at an electricity generator and distributor, and a Design Engineer and Construction Supervisor in a city council.

Graham is a Foundation Fellow of the Australian Institute of Company Directors, a Fellow of the Australian Institute of Management, and a Member of the U.S. Academy of Management.

INTELLECTUAL PROPERTY RIGHTS

A Unique System

By reading this book you have access to a business system that contains a wealth of ideas and methods. You will benefit from our company's many years of experience in consulting, training and software development.

While patents have been applied for on certain aspects of the Strategic Factor System, we invite you to use the System except in the applications below.

Restricted Applications

There are Patents Pending in the USA and Australia on the core steps of the Strategic Factor System. All rights are reserved in relation to this System.

The following applications require a written license from our company, Strategic Factors Pty Ltd ACN 001 625 958. These especially pertain to *consultancy* and *software uses*.

- providing consultancy services that use the System, in whole or in part;

- retaining consultancy services that use the System, in whole or in part;

- providing consultancy services to an organization that uses the System, in whole or in part, to assist it to employ the System;

- developing software or computer systems to use the System, in whole or in part;

- enabling or adapting existing software or computer systems to use the System, in whole or in part;

- enabling or adapting existing software or computer systems, which may follow an alternative method, to use the System, in whole or in part;

- distributing the System, in whole or in part, via software or computer systems;

- using the System to develop any material and transferring that material in whole or in part to software or computer systems.

Licensing

Strategic Factors Pty Ltd may license the use of the System for commercial purposes, subject to agreement on appropriate terms.

License requests can be made on-line, by fax or post to:

Strategic Factors
PO Box 702
Mosman NSW 2088
Australia
Fax: (Sydney) 612 9969 2596
E-mail: admin@strategicfactors.com
Website: www.strategicfactors.com

CHAPTER 1

A NEW WAY OF THINKING

In spite of all the books and articles written over the past three decades, organizations still confuse process activity with strategic success.

Ask any manager what makes his or her organization successful and you'll get a description of internal activity rather than the precise results of this activity. And you know, that manager would be wrong!

Take, for example, the private hospital that lists, as its critical success factors, "capital development, responsible financial management, developing key partnerships, quality models of care, efficient systems and working together." What we have here is a catalog of *internal processes* and, as praiseworthy and as well-performed as they might be, they are *not* what determines the success of the hospital. They are not *outcomes*.

Or, as another example, take the electricity-generating organization that lists key result areas as what makes it successful. These KRA's include "resource management, environmental responsibility and people." Again, we have internal processes and *vague domains of activity* that are not the keys to the electricity organization's success, are not *outcomes*.

OUTSIDE IN, NOT INSIDE OUT

Why are managers so clearly unable to identify the essential ingredients of their organization's success? The answer is that they insist on looking at their performance from the *inside out*, rather than the *outside in*. It's that simple!

We're like the fly in the honey. We become entrapped by our own organization. We become weighed down by policies, procedures, systems, processes, practices and they become our world. What's worse, they become *the* world. And, like the fly in the honey, we can't escape. If we're not careful, we become blinded to reality, the reality of what it takes to be successful.

So just what are those few things around which organizational activity must focus and which lead to success? The answer is strategic factors! They're discovered by looking at your organization's (or business unit's) performance from the *outside in*. By seeing yourself as your customers, suppliers, employees, owners and others see you, and asking: how do *they* evaluate our performance? What do *they* look for from us?

We insist on looking at our performance from the inside out, rather than the outside in.

That's when you move from the inner realm to the outer. That's when you take *their* perspective, not yours. That's when you stand in their shoes, not your own. And they are very different shoes!

So what are strategic factors?

DEFINING STRATEGIC FACTORS

Strategic factors are those things that your organization or business unit needs to get right in order to succeed with your key stakeholders, that is, your customers, suppliers, employees, owners and any other organization, business unit or individual that you depend on for success. The stakeholders use these criteria to evaluate you.

Examples of Strategic Factors. Chapter 3 onwards offers numerous examples of these strategic factors. For customers, the strategic factors are customer service, product quality and the like. With employees, they are items such as rewards, company reputation and job security. For owners in a public company, the strategic factors include dividends and capital growth.

Strategic Factors as Common Currency. Strategic factors provide not only a pathway to success but also a common currency that links the way in which strategic planning and performance measurement are undertaken. The key word is *link,* and strategic factors form that link.

Strategic Factors across Sectors. Strategic factors also provide the tools to be able to address the needs not just of private sector profit-seeking organizations, but also of non-profit organizations from both the public and private sectors. Here again strategic factors act as integrators because all organizations have them at their core.

Strategic Factors for Business Units. Strategic factors also provide the way to move across the terrain from corporate to department, from organization to business unit. Because they apply just as well to a unit's relationship to key stakeholders, they make it easy to link the unit's strategic plan to the organization's.

> **Strategic factors supply us with a system for tying all the diverse strategy concepts and activities together.**

Strategic Factor System. Finally, strategic factors supply us with a system for streamlining strategy development and its measurement, a system for tying all the diverse strategy concepts and activities together. We call it the Strategic Factor System.

RESULTS FROM EMPLOYING STRATEGIC FACTORS

Figure 1.1 lists the results you'll achieve by reading this book and applying its ideas.

Perhaps in reviewing the column on the left-hand side, you may identify some of the problems you've been experiencing in your own organization or business unit. Have you, for instance, experienced confusion in defining competitive advantage? Have you found difficulty in developing strategy for all your key stakeholders? Are you able to differentiate and position your organization or business unit effectively? Have you found that your key performance indicators are rarely strategy-driven?

Now run your eyes down the right-hand column. Wouldn't it be great to be able to avoid the problems on the left and achieve the results on the right? On the completion of this book, you will.

As Figure 1.1 suggests, you'll be able to connect strategic analysis and strategy formulation. You'll be able to write

Figure 1.1   **Results of Employing Strategic Factors**

Without Strategic Factors	With Strategic Factors
Connecting strategic analysis and strategy formulation	
Ranges from poorly connected to completely disconnected	Connection clear and streamlined
Defining competitive advantage	
Gets mixed up with internal capabilities	Defined outside-in, not inside-out
Conducting competitive assessments and assessing competitive advantage	
Lacks focus on external factors	Focuses squarely on external factors
Establishing clear and quantified objectives	
Generally a jumble of statements	Clear statements built around measurable outcomes
Writing clear and focused strategy	
Lacks focus, as methods are confused	Clearly focused, as method is clear
Developing strategy for key stakeholders	
Tends to focus on customers to the exclusion of other key stakeholders	Encompasses *all* key stakeholders
Developing strategy for non-profit organizations and for business units	
Difficult, as most techniques are designed for profit organizations and not for business units	No difficulties, as the techniques can apply across all organizations and business units
Defining value	
Mixes cost with "value added"	Value clearly defined
Defining differentiation and positioning	
Imprecise and not well related	Linked and complementary
Developing strategy for lobbying, acquisitions, strategic alliances and innovation	
Frequently seen as "add-ons" and are poorly integrated	Clearly linked to competitive advantage

Linking strategy formulation and performance measurement

Hazy linkage or no linkage at all   Intimately linked

Developing key performance indicators

Rarely strategy-driven   Always strategy-driven

clear and quantified objectives. You'll be able to define competitive advantage clearly and conduct an effective competitive assessment. You'll be able to write clear and focused strategy for all your key stakeholders — not just customers, but suppliers, employees, owners and all those who make your organization a success. If your focus is a non-profit organization or a business unit, you'll be able to develop strategy easily. You'll be able to explore the full range of strategic options, such as lobbying, acquisitions, alliances and innovation. You'll be able to link strategy formulation and performance measurement.

You'll be able to connect strategic planning to performance measurement as never before.

THE BOOK FROM HERE ON

The chapters are organized around a series of steps. These are illustrated in Figure 1.2.

Chapter 2, "Your Foundation Stones," shows how to identify the key stakeholders of your organization or business unit and distinguish between stakeholders and *key* stakeholders. The chapter gives examples from a variety of industries.

Chapter 3, "At the Cutting Edge," contains a detailed definition of strategic factors and provides examples for customers, again from a variety of industries. This chapter forms the basis for the rest of the book.

Chapter 4, "It's Wise to Analyze — Strategically," extends

Figure 1.2   Sequence of Steps and Chapters

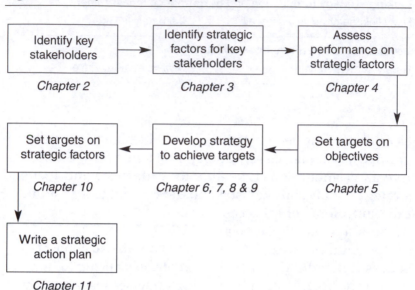

the identification of strategic factors to *all* key stakeholders, outlining steps for undertaking strategic analysis and explaining each in detail. It provides you with five ways of identifying strategic factors for your organization or business unit. Two specific tools, the Competitive Assessment Matrix and the Competitive Advantage Profile, are detailed. There are also lists of key strategic issues from a number of organizations, derived from strategic analysis.

Chapter 5, "Where Are You Going?" shows an innovative way to set objectives classified by key stakeholder. The chapter also shows how to quantify these objectives by setting key performance indicators on them and then establishing targets for these indicators.

Chapter 6, "The Fatal Flaw," provides an expanded definition of the term "competitors," and a new way of defining "competitive advantage," based on strategic factors. It is distinguished from internal capabilities. The concepts *value, differentiation* and *positioning* are also shown to be based on strategic factors and are demonstrated through a number of examples. The chapter shows how competitive advantage, value, differentiation and positioning are linked, and how each concept can be employed in developing strategy.

Chapter 7, "Doing What You Do Better," demonstrates how to design winning strategy by following Scale Strategy, one of what we call Strategy's Three S's. The chapter also demonstrates the importance of developing competitive advantage at key points in the value chain of your industry.

Chapter 8, "Why Diversification Is Not a Strategy," tackles the second of our Three S's, Scope Strategy. It shows that while most organizations are lost when it comes to diversification, it needn't be this way — so long as diversification is approached via knowledge of strategic factors.

Chapter 9, "Avoiding Naive Strategy," elaborates the third S in our Three S's, Structure Strategy. Here we discuss four options: lobbying, strategic alliance, acquisition and innovation — all linked to strategic factors. Also presented are examples of organizations employing these options.

Chapter 10, "Tracking Strategy in Real Time," shows that while we are able to track strategy by the extent to which it delivers results on objectives (the subject of Chapter 5), there is an extended way of measuring the success of strategy: producing leading indicators by tracking results on strategic factors.

Chapter 11, "The Need for Action," provides guidelines to follow in developing your strategic plan and discusses seven common mistakes. In providing remedies, special emphasis is placed on the importance of action planning.

Chapter 12, "Outside Looking In," stresses the importance of taking an outside-in view of the performance of your organization or business unit. Only when you do this, the chapter concludes, can you take your key stakeholders' perspectives. The chapter summarizes the major steps in this book and provides examples of the benefits clients tell us they receive from following these steps.

There are three appendices to round out the book. These are concerned with the difference between strategic and operational plans, board involvement in strategic planning, and competitive advantage along value chains.

Finally, there is a glossary. As in all management fields, terms abound. It has been the aim in this book to limit their number to those that are essential.

TRY THIS

Position your organization or business unit on the twelve results listed in Figure 1.1. If you find yourself on the right hand side on all twelve, please get in touch — we should talk! If, on the other hand — and this is the more likely result — you do some of those things reasonably well and others either poorly or not at all, then this book is for you.

The exercise will also help you determine which chapters most need your attention.

CHAPTER 2

YOUR FOUNDATION STONES

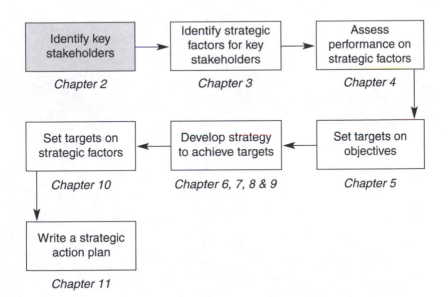

The starting point for correctly identifying strategic factors and developing successful strategies is knowing who your key stakeholders are. Many organizations don't, and they busily work away, ever improving processes and wondering why success eludes them.

Other organizations recognize stakeholders, but fail to focus on those that are *key*. They then become distracted by all and sundry, their resources become scattered and, like the proverbial shotgun, they miss their target.

Another group pays lip service to key stakeholders, but their real focus is customers, customers, customers. Now customers are *key*, but they're not the *only* key stakeholders.

Toyota and McDonald's recognize a diverse range of stakeholders and develop sharp and focused strategy for suppliers, for example. They know that they can't produce effective outcomes for their customers unless they first produce effective outcomes for suppliers. They also recognize that both of these key stakeholders depend on the successful implementation of employee strategy.

We avoid either having too broad or too narrow a focus in our System, as will be demonstrated in this chapter.

> **The starting point for correctly identifying strategic factors and developing successful strategies is knowing who your key stakeholders are.**

Key stakeholders *are* important because they provide resources to an organization or business unit through the transactions that take place between them and the organization.

The importance of strategic factors lies in the fact that they underpin these transactions.

TRANSACTIONS AND KEY STAKEHOLDERS

All organizations and business units engage in such transactions. Figure 2.1 presents four typical stakeholders: customers, suppliers, employees and owners. However, the

Figure 2.1 **Transactions and Key Stakeholders**

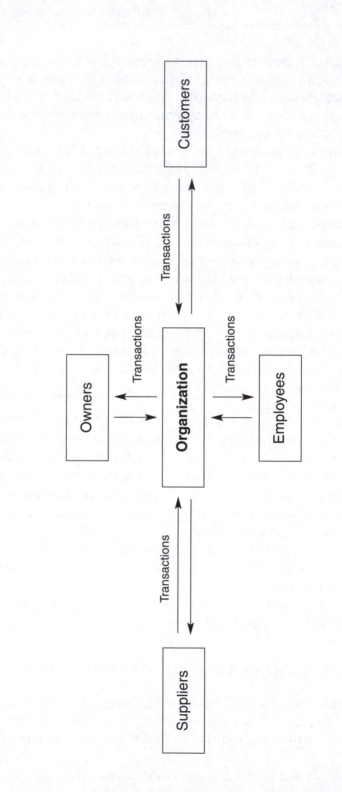

number and variety of stakeholders in any particular situation is more complex than shown in this diagram.

The arrows in Figure 2.1 represent transactions: exchanges of something for something else. Customers receive goods and services and, in return, transmit money to an organization or business unit. Suppliers supply goods and services and, in return, receive funds. Employees put effort into an organization's performance and, in return, receive a salary. Owners supply funds and, in return, expect dividends and capital growth.

All organizations and business units can be analyzed in this way. Their purpose is to reap benefit from these relationships and the transactions therein. Take, for instance, the case of customers: while an organization naturally wishes to provide goods and services to customer specifications, it won't do it for nothing. In fact, one objective of that relationship is to obtain the maximum return to the organization from the supply of these goods and services.

In the case of suppliers: here the transactions are concerned with obtaining a supply of goods and services and paying for them in such a way as to accrue maximum benefit to the purchasing organization.

A business or government organization is not a social club, designed purely for the benefit of employees. But, at the other extreme, exploitation of employees would be quite counter-productive, as far as the organization is concerned, in the long term. Thus, the transactions between an organization and its employees need to be balanced between the latter's expectations and the organization's need to reap maximum benefit.

When we come to the relationship between an organization and its owners, the latter expect their "pound of flesh" in return for their investment. However, the organization itself and, hopefully, the owners, too, understand that there are limitations on the returns that can be paid — some funds need to be retained for future growth and development.

A clear grasp of the relationships between an organization and its stakeholders and, especially, of the relevant transactions, will lead to a much sharper way of thinking about strategy.

KEY STAKEHOLDERS AS SOURCES OF STRATEGY

In developing strategy, we focus on stakeholders who are *key*.

We define *key stakeholders* as *organizations, business units, and people with whom an organization or business unit interacts and on whom it depends for success.*

Success requires that strategy pays heed to the needs of all key stakeholders.

Furthermore, the success of your organization or unit does not depend simply on emphasizing the needs of *one* key stakeholder, e.g. the shareholders, to the exclusion of all others. Success requires that strategy for your organization or business unit pays heed to the needs of *all* its key stakeholders and balances them.

The emphasis is on *key* stakeholders. Organizations and business units have a good number and variety of stakeholders, but there will usually emerge a core set who have a fundamental impact. These are the *key stakeholders.*

The following four examples of key stakeholders come from organizations that we have assisted in their strategic planning. While real organizations, their names have been changed.

SALEM PRIVATE HOSPITAL

Salem Private Hospital is part of a much larger public hospital founded by an order of religious nuns. While the nuns now play little part in the day-to-day running of the hospital, the philosophy of the religious order still permeates the values of the hospital itself. These values include working together, developing key partnerships, positive community relations and quality models of care.

As part of a strategic planning exercise and in preparation for developing effective strategy, the planning team of the hospital identified the hospital's key stakeholders as:

- Patients
- Specialists
- Staff
- Health funds
- Suppliers
- General practitioners
- Parent organization

Most of these are what we would expect and need no explanation, but some terms might be unfamiliar. Specialists are those doctors who specialize, for example, in heart surgery or cancer treatment and who have their own practices. They work for the hospital on a consultancy basis for their particular patients.

Staff include nurses, nursing aids and other hospital employees, as well as doctors employed by Salem Private. Health funds are those organizations with whom patients take out health insurance. Health funds pay the hospital on their behalf for surgery and other services. General practitioners are doctors who have their own private practice and who recommend to their patients a particular hospital. Lastly, parent organization refers to the fact that Salem Private Hospital is a division within the larger public hospital.

This private hospital recognises the need to develop effective strategy for each of its key stakeholders as well as to identify the relevant strategic factors.

MONTGOMERY STATE LIBRARY

The running of a private hospital is complex and so, too, is the running of a modern state library. Clients these days demand electronic access to worldwide information.

This government-owned, 350-employee organization has set itself a number of challenges. These include:

- To transform the delivery of information and information services required by customers by unlocking the resources of the State collection and other worldwide information sources

- To develop a successful integrated library network to deliver enhanced information services to clients

- To provide clients with an outstanding State collection by acquiring, organizing and preserving published and original material

- To be an active and innovative cultural institution, delivering dynamic, professional events and programs

- To be recognised as one of the great libraries of the world; a distinctive, welcoming and functional information and cultural center

- To create a supportive environment that enables the best possible use of all resources in order to satisfy user needs

The strategic planning team from Montgomery State Library realized that these goals could only be met through effective strategy. So the strategic planning team set about identifying the library's key stakeholders. Here is its list:

- State Government as owner
- Corporates
- Individual consumers (end users)
- Donors and sponsors
- Staff
- Suppliers and contractors

Being a government-owned organization, the library needs to identify the State Government as a key stakeholder. Its customers are of two types. Corporates are those organizations that employ the services of the library. Individual consumers are those within those corporates who ultimately use the library services and those individuals who access the library directly.

The library also depends for its funding on donors and sponsors. While the State Government provides the bulk of its funds, Montgomery State Library seeks to raise funds from individual and corporate donors and sponsors, nonetheless. Its emphasis is to make this a growing funding stream.

Staff are, of course, the employees of the library. These include current employees and potential employees, the latter being those the library wishes to attract now and in the future. Suppliers and contractors are those organizations and individuals providing goods and services.

Having identified the library's key stakeholders, the planning team then sought to understand the strategic factors relevant to each, with a view to developing effective strategy for each.

COMMUNITY SUPPORT SERVICES

Developing strategy as well as understanding key stake-holders and strategic factors applies to the not-for-profit sector just as much as it does to the profit and government sectors. Community Support Services is a church-based organization that provides assistance to those in need.

It conducts a number of programs such as the supported accommodation assistance programs, disability programs, family programs, community child care centers, child care inclusion programs and prison ministry. Its vision is "to enact the Gospel by being bearers of hope, agents of change and builders of community, enabling people to live, grow and develop with dignity, in life-enriching relationships."

In embracing this vision, it depends very much on government funding for its activities.

Community Support Services sees as its key stakeholders:

- Owners
- Fund-providers
- Employees
- Donors

- Volunteers
- Customers
- Government as regulator
- Government as service provider

The owner is the church that founded the organization, while the government is the major provider of ongoing funding for programs. Further funds are provided by donors. Human resources to run the organization come from volunteers as well as employees.

Customers, and this was the term preferred by the organization (not clients or recipients), are individuals who pay for their services and others who do not.

The government occupies two roles in this situation: first as regulator and second as service provider. It's important in identifying key stakeholders to recognise the different roles that they may play, because various roles give rise to different strategic factors. Government as regulator holds different expectations from government as service provider; hence the strategic factors are different. As regulator the Government expects Community Support Services to stay within the rules. As service provider, it expects it to use government services appropriately.

DYNAMIC CONNECTORS

Dynamic Connectors is a privately-owned company that supplies its corporate customers with a comprehensive range of electronic connections to suit a broad spectrum of industry applications. These include automation networks, broad band networks, customer premises and electronic connections.

Automation networks involve the building of communication systems for automation, operating through various transmission media. Dynamic Connectors provides electronic connectors for those applications. It also provides connectors for broad band networks. These include connecting solutions for voice, data and video networks. In the case of customer premises, Dynamic Connectors is concerned with providing telecommunication and cabling infrastructure (in copper and fiber). Customers here operate in environments described as corporate, industrial, manufacturing, educational, retail and small or home office.

As a specialized niche player, Dynamic Connectors identified a small group of key stakeholders. These are:

- Customers
- Suppliers
- Employees
- Shareholders

The customers are those organizations referred to in the descriptions above. Dynamic Connectors' suppliers are companies that provide it with the wiring and other means to facilitate the connections. Employees are, of course, those individuals that work for Dynamic Connectors, while the shareholders are the private investors who own the company.

Dynamic Connectors understands the importance of clearly identifying its *key* stakeholders. It knows that effective strategy depends on this successful identification. It also knows that successful strategy depends on correctly identifying the strategic factors for each of these four stakeholders.

What we see from these examples is the importance of *correctly identifying the key stakeholders of an organization or business unit*. This leads to a further identification, that of strategic factors — which, in turn, leads to the development of effective strategy.

MORE EXAMPLES OF THE STAKEHOLDER APPROACH

British Telecom uses stakeholder consultation to ascertain the views of a wide range of stakeholders concerning their ethical expectations. It conducts discussions with its consumers and convenes seminars and conferences on key issues. Describing this stakeholder consultation as the means by which commercial success is achieved, British Telecom calls it the way to keep the organization on the right track.

The Cooperative Bank, also in the United Kingdom, describes its stakeholders as "partners." Interestingly, it commissions independently audited reports on its performance with each of its key stakeholders.

Novo Nordisk, which is a large Danish company in the chemicals and biotechnology field, also focuses on key stakeholders in developing its plans for business success.

Another example comes from the US publishing field. Here, Berrett-Koehler Publishers applies a stakeholder approach to corporate governance. The firm has identified as key stakeholders its authors, suppliers, customers, marketers, distributors and employees. It has developed a formal mechanism for incorporating the viewpoints of external stakeholders. Through "stakeholder councils" a dialogue is established between Berrett-Koehler and its key stakeholders.

Coca-Cola recognizes the diversity of its key stakeholders and their impact on strategy. Management believes that it needs to anticipate their concerns so as to develop appropriate strategies and protect the company's reputation.

The whole process of developing strategy becomes more manageable when you break your organization's environment into identifiable key stakeholders.

Similarly, Elf Aquitaine, the largest oil company in France, acknowledges the impact that key stakeholders have on its future and strategic planning.

These are but a few of the numerous organizations that take their key stakeholders seriously and develop strategy for all of them.

KEY STAKEHOLDERS AS FOUNDATIONS

This chapter has sought to demonstrate why key stakeholders are the base on which successful strategy is built. In the cases of Salem Private Hospital, Montgomery State Library, Community Support Services and Dynamic Connectors, we saw lists of key stakeholders from a variety of industries. We noticed how they varied and how the descriptions are industry specific. To blandly label all stakeholders "customers" or group them under a general "customer perspective," as some authorities suggest, runs the risk of missing special differences between key stakeholders. Look at the key stakeholders of Salem Private Hospital, for example, and notice their labels and diversity.

As the rest of this book demonstrates, the whole process of developing strategy becomes more manageable when you break your organization's environment into identifiable key stakeholders. Each can then be taken in turn and relevant strategy developed.

What strategic factors are and why their identification is so important is the subject of the next chapter.

CHAPTER 3

AT THE
CUTTING EDGE

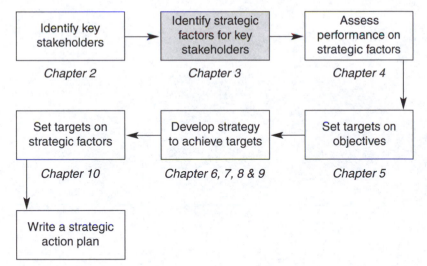

As key stakeholders are your foundation stone, strategic factors are your cutting edge. Organizations that do not clearly understand their strategic factors are like a blunt knife. They have no penetration and they certainly don't do the job.

We see "blunt" organizations all around us. And, dare I say, many of them are large and often government-owned. Organizations like these operate in a haze through which employee effort is dissipated. Everyone is busy, but to what effect?

The answer to this waste of effort on the part of employees has often been to write a strategic plan. That will fix things up! But the plan itself becomes a flabby document, full of vague but high-sounding statements that, in the end, take the organization nowhere.

This is not to suggest that writing a strategic plan shouldn't be undertaken, but it is to suggest that the plan must be incisive. (In Chapter 11 we take up the question of strategic plan mistakes.) And you can't have an incisive strategic plan without a precise understanding of strategic factors.

Obtaining this understanding is the subject of this chapter.

STRATEGIC FACTORS IN TRANSACTIONS

Figure 3.1 is a modified version of Figure 2.1. In it the word "transactions" has been replaced by a description of the nature of those transactions. For example, in the case of employees, they supply their "effort" and in return receive "strategic factors for employees." So while strategy development starts with an identification of the key stakeholders relevant to an organization or business unit, it is built around an understanding of the strategic factors applicable to each key stakeholder.

Let's look at this Figure 3.1 more closely. Arrows leading from the organization to each of the key stakeholders — customers, owners, suppliers and employees — represent the

Figure 3.1 **Strategic Factors for Key Stakeholders**

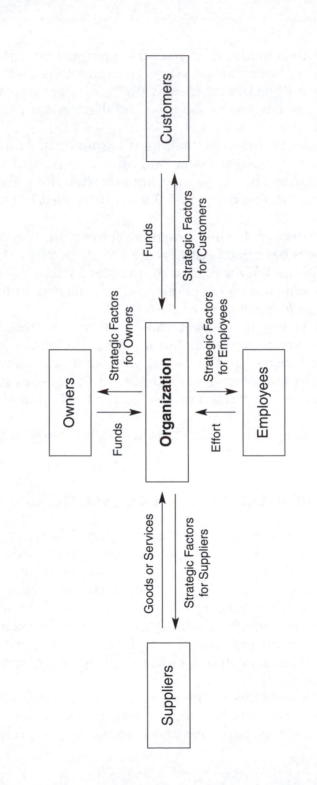

strategic factors relevant to them. Performance on these factors is what they receive.

The organization receives something in return, of course. In the case of customers, it receives funds as payments. In the case of owners, it also receives funds as investments. From suppliers, the organization receives goods or services. From employees, it receives effort.

Obviously, no organization can operate without goods or services, funds, and effort. But receiving all these in abundance depends on the strategic factors.

We label them *factors* because they are major components of the transactions; we label them *strategic* because they are the basis on which an organization or business unit builds strategy in our System.

Strategic factors are, as we have stressed, factors that are critical to the success of an organization. But they are different from the commonly used "critical success factors." Strategic factors are externally focused, as can be seen above, whereas the term "critical success factors" covers a range of items that includes internal processes, such as manufacturing and training, and results, such as revenue.

You should also note that there is no such thing as a *single* set of strategic factors for an organization or business unit; they are always specific to a key stakeholder. Figure 3.1 shows four sets of strategic factors clearly illustrated, not one.

There is no such thing as a single set of strategic factors for an organization or business unit.

The examples in the rest of this chapter are concerned with one key stakeholder, the customer. Focusing on a single key stakeholder type enables a better understanding of the concept of strategic factors than were we to be switching between types. In later chapters, we will consider strategic factors for key stakeholders other than customers.

7-ELEVEN

7-Eleven convenience stores are found in many suburbs and towns and carry a range of essential items, such as milk and bread; they are "conveniently" located for a local population. In the retail marketplace they occupy a niche quite different from that of the supermarket.

The 7-Eleven convenience store is a classic example of a small business that has many of the attributes of the large ones. It has customers, employees, owners, and other key stakeholders.

The six strategic factors relevant to the relationship of a 7-Eleven store with its *customers* are listed in Figure 3.2. Also listed are the benefits that the latter derive from each of these strategic factors.

Figure 3.2   Strategic Factors and Customer Benefits in a 7-Eleven Store

Strategic Factors	Customer Benefits
Location	Lower travel costs; ease of parking
Hours of operation	Open when needed
Customer service	Pleasant staff, able to give good advice and knowledgeable about stock
Range of goods sold	Plenty of choice from wide range of goods
Store presentation	Attractively laid out to make shopping pleasant; easy-to-find products; speedy shopping; clean and hygienic
Price	Savings

The strategic factors emerge when we picture a potential customer driving down the street and making the decision to stop at a convenience store. He or she weighs up the customer benefits listed in Figure 3.2 that each strategic factor delivers.

So let's look closely at the decision-making process. The first thing that the driver might weigh up is where the store is located. Is it on a busy road? Can I park right outside the store? Or do I have to walk a considerable distance after parking the car? These and other questions concerning location will be on the driver's mind.

Next comes consideration of the hours of operation: Is the store open now? Are its hours 9 am to 5 pm, or is it open 24 hours a day?

The question of customer service looms large: Are the staff pleasant? Are they abrupt or offhand? Do they know what they're selling? Is the service fast?

There are other factors to be weighed up as well, such as the variety of goods sold. Does this store carry only a narrow range of goods, so that I will have to go to another store to get everything I need? Or is it a one-stop shop? What about its presentation? Is it clean? Is it tidy? Is it well laid-out? Can I find the items easily?

Finally, the driver considers price and asks: Is its pricing competitive? This doesn't mean, of course, that a convenience store has to be the cheapest around. Far from it. But it does have to be competitive with the other choices available to the driver.

The driver's final assessment is a trade-off of one strategic factor against another.

A set of strategic factors such as those in Figure 3.2 could also be developed for other key stakeholders of a 7-Eleven convenience store, such as owners, suppliers and employees.

STRATEGIC FACTORS IN DETAIL

Strategic factors have the following characteristics:

- They are externally focused.
- They relate to stakeholder expectations.
- They are driven by internal processes and capabilities.
- They are factors which an organization or business unit has to handle well in order to succeed.
- They are the criteria used by stakeholders to assess an organization's or business unit's performance.

Let's examine the six factors for convenience store customer benefits (Figure 3.2) against the characteristics outlined above.

Strategic factors are externally focused. It's very easy to view performance inside out — a point made in Chapter 1. We become trapped by our systems, processes and procedures. When this occurs, we miss the relevant strategic factors. These are found by looking outside in; in other words strategic factors are discovered by becoming externally focused.

What is not listed under strategic factors are internal processes and capabilities.

For example, a selection process that assists 7-Eleven to select the right staff to deal effectively with customers may enable it to lift its performance on the strategic factor of customer service. However, such an internal process is not a strategic factor in itself.

Strategic factors relate to stakeholder expectations. Note how the six factors for 7-Eleven relate to customer expectations. Assume you are a potential customer of a convenience store: don't you expect the store to get the six strategic factors right, even to a minimal extent?

Strategic factors are driven by internal processes and capabilities. The 7-Eleven store's strategic factors would be driven by internal processes and capabilities, such as advertising and well-trained staff. Yet these processes and capabilities, as I have said, would not themselves be strategic factors for customers. Customers don't care about advertising and staff training. They only care what advertising and staff training achieve for them. In other words, they only perceive the *impact* of advertising and staff training when these procedures surface as strategic factors — as store image and good customer service. As Figure 3.3 demonstrates, there is a significant difference between the wording of internal processes/capabilities and strategic factors.

Figure 3.3   **Internal Processes and Capabilities versus Strategic Factors**

Internal Processes and Capabilities

- Advertising (process)
- Well-trained staff (capability)
- Up-to-date computer system (capability)
- Training (process)
- Product development (process)
- High-quality manufacture (capability)
- Efficient production (capability)

Strategic Factors

- Image
- Customer Service
- Delivery
- Customer Service
- Range of Products
- Product Quality
- Price

An organization or business unit has to do well on strategic factors in order to succeed. Let's suppose the 7-Eleven store has five of the factors in place, but its location makes it inaccessible. The store will be unsuccessful. Suppose it has everything in place except customer service. Employees are rude and do not know their products. Again, it will be unsuccessful. Suppose that the other five factors are in place, but the prices are so high that people are deterred from becoming customers. Again, that store will be unsuccessful. The example illustrates how, for customers, the six listed strategic factors are all crucial.

Strategic factors are the decision criteria used by stakeholders to assess an organization's performance. In the case of the 7-Eleven store, customers weigh up location, hours of operation, customer service, range of goods sold, store presentation and price and make a decision to go to one convenience store rather than another.

In fact, the key to discovering strategic factors is to put ourselves in the shoes of our key stakeholders and figure out how they decide to choose our organization or business unit over others. Alternatively, and better still, we ask *them*. How to do this is

Strategic factors are the decision criteria used by stakeholders to assess an organization's performance.

explained in Chapter 4.

Now let's move on to consider strategic factors for customers in a variety of industries. These three examples come from organizations we have assisted in their strategic planning (names have been changed).

BIRMINGHAM BANK

This example concerns business units that are within the same industry — in fact, from the same organization, Birmingham Bank, and from the same division within that organization — but which have different strategic factors for their customers. The division is the Financial Markets Group (Figure 3.4). The first of the three business units within that division is the Money Market Unit.

Figure 3.4   **Organization Chart of Units within Birmingham Bank**

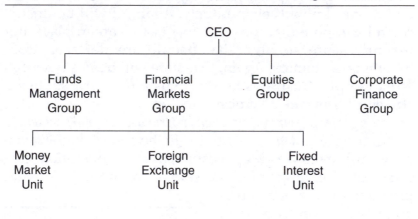

Money Market Unit

The customers of the Money Market Unit are organizations that might borrow $10 million for terms from overnight to three years. (Loans for more than the three-year term fall within the Fixed Interest Unit's area; see next example.) The strategic factors relevant to this unit's customers are:

- Price
- Perception of bank
- Customer service
- Bank's accessibility
- Good outcomes for customers
- Range of products

Again, we see the existence of price and customer service as strategic factors, but we need to remember that the definition of both these factors in this case is quite different from that of a software developer, a nickel refiner or a 7-Eleven store. In addition, we see the emergence of other factors that are peculiar to this unit and the banking industry, for example, "perception of bank." This item refers to the way in which customers regard its security and innovation.

These six strategic factors are the criteria used by customers to decide whether to use the Money Market Unit or go to the competition. They are, therefore, an essential launching pad for developing customer strategy.

Fixed Interest Unit

The Fixed Interest Unit within the same division (Figure 3.4) organizes loans for terms longer than three years and issues securities on behalf of clients. These securities include domestic bonds and commercial paper, transferable loan certificates and various securitized issues. The strategic factors relevant for its customers are:

- Price
- Customer service
- Range of products
- Bank's reputation

The dynamics of this unit's relationship with its customers are clearly reflected in its strategic factors. The bank's reputation is of great importance, as is price, customer service and the range of products that the unit makes available. We can see how these strategic factors are externally focused and relate to the needs of customers, who would use them as criteria for the decision to go with the Fixed Interest Unit or its competition.

Foreign Exchange Unit

The Foreign Exchange Unit acts as an interbank market-maker in foreign exchange and offers foreign exchange advisory and execution services. The strategic factors for the customers of this unit are:

- Price
- Range of products
- Customer service
- Accessibility
- Settlements
- Credit rating/brand recognition

While some of the factors above are on the lists for the Money Market and Fixed Interest Units, there are also differences, such as "settlements" and "credit rating/brand recognition." These variations emerge because the transactions that the Foreign Exchange Unit has with its customers obviously differ from those of the other two units. Again, we can see that the strategic factors are externally focused, relating to stakeholder expectations, although they are driven by internal processes and practices.

If the unit performs badly on any of these strategic factors, its customers will go to the competition.

The starting point for all three units to develop customer strategy are the same: their lists of strategic factors.

REXEL SOLUTIONS

Rexel Solutions produces software for patent attorneys, who handle the registration and management of intellectual property such as patents, trademarks and designs. It has client sites in twelve different countries and provides a comprehensive suite of software that addresses attorneys' professional and clerical needs.

The software assists clients in the processing of all property and case types. It also provides a comprehensive client relationship management data base and has a number of automatic calculation features. For example, it calculates due dates and reminders for the patent and trademark process and automatically generates forms, letters, charges and official fees.

In the main, Rexel Solutions' customers are the patent attorneys themselves and its strategic planning team identified the following strategic factors as appropriate to them:

- Price
- Customer service
- Product quality
- Functionality
- Range of services
- Delivery and support
- Image and reputation

While price was seen as an important factor, Rexel in no way aimed to be the cheapest in the industry. In fact, their product was a highly sophisticated and expensive one. One of the main features of customer service was responsiveness, and the essential ingredients of product quality were consistency and freedom from faults. The strategic factor of functionality refers to the requirement that the software must deliver what it promises. Lastly, image and reputation are seen as important for a product that is difficult for customers to evaluate. The dimensions of image and reputation considered to be relevant were Rexel Solutions' credibility, knowledge and financial stability.

CALEDONIA NICKEL

Caledonia Nickel is a public company. It produces nickel ingots, which its customers incorporate into other products, such as stainless steel. Thus the customers of the refiner are themselves industrial organizations.

Five strategic factors exist for customers in this industry:

- Product quality
- Price
- Reliability of supply
- Range of products
- Customer service

If you compare this list with the previous one for Rexel Solutions, you'll see that product quality, price and customer service are common to both. The definitions of these strategic factors are, however, quite different. Product quality in the nickel-refining industry is quite different from product quality in the software industry. The same is true of customer service.

Moreover, in the case of Caledonia Nickel, another two factors have entered the list of strategic factors: "range of products" and "reliability of supply." Regarding the first, customers expect the refiner to produce a sufficiently large range of products for their needs to be met from a single source. As to the second, highly geared as they are to supply, industrial organizations must be confident of 100% reliability.

You need to know how a key stakeholder makes the decision to support you rather than the competition.

Note how these strategic factors comply with the definition. They are not a description of internal processes and practices. The internal processes managed by the nickel refiner are of little interest to its customers. What is important in order to be successful is doing well on these five strategic factors. If Caledonia Nickel falls down on reliability of supply or product quality or customer service or price or range of products, it will start to lose contracts.

STEPS TOWARDS A WINNING STRATEGY

Knowing the strategic factors relevant to your key stakeholders is the platform that allows you to progress to superior performance on these factors (Figure 3.5). And this excellent performance must be achieved for *each* of your key stakeholders.

Figure 3.5   **Platform for Success**

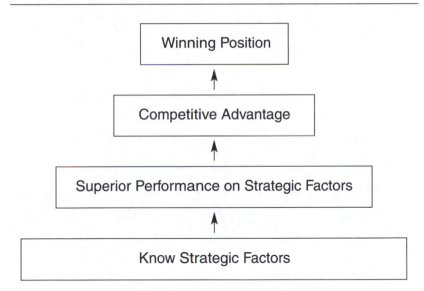

High quality performance on strategic factors can only lead to competitive advantage. Of course, once this is achieved, you will have attained a winning position.

The message in this chapter is clear: you cannot have a winning strategy unless you focus your attention on the strategic factors relevant to your key stakeholders. So you must first identify those key stakeholders, those people who determine the destiny of your organization or business unit. Guided by their expectations, they engage in transactions, and the extent to which these transactions are "profitable" for both your organization and the key stakeholders will determine the extent to which you prosper.

It is in the characteristics of these transactions that strategic factors lie. You will discover them by putting yourself in your key stakeholders' shoes. Alternatively, and even better, ask the key stakeholders directly.

The answers you get become the foundation for the strategy developed for each key stakeholder.

CHAPTER 4

IT'S WISE TO ANALYZE — STRATEGICALLY

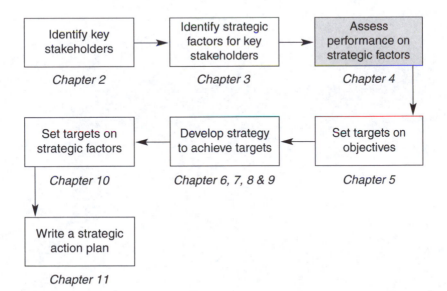

Identify key stakeholders	Identify strategic factors for key stakeholders	Assess performance on strategic factors
Chapter 2	*Chapter 3*	*Chapter 4*

Set targets on strategic factors	Develop strategy to achieve targets	Set targets on objectives
Chapter 10	*Chapter 6, 7, 8 & 9*	*Chapter 5*

Write a strategic action plan
Chapter 11

Strategic factors, properly identified and clearly articulated, become the pathways to incisive strategies. Along those pathways sits strategic analysis.

It's noticeable in our consulting work that "analysis" is not a topic that generates great enthusiasm. It sounds like hard work. "Let's just get on with it," people think. But the danger in just getting on with it without appropriate and effective analysis is that your strategies will be driven by pet projects, hidden agendas and just plain bias. The result can be disastrous.

Perhaps one of the reasons that members of planning teams shy away from analysis is the way it's done. In most cases the analysis ends up divorced from the strategy developed. As you know from Chapter 1, our aim is to link strategic analysis to strategy development via strategic factors.

In this chapter we show you how, via these six steps:

1. Form a planning team.

2. Profile competitors.

3. Identify strategic factors in your industry.

4. Complete a Competitive Assessment Matrix on strategic factors.

5. Develop a Competitive Advantage Profile around strategic factors, for each product/service.

6. Summarize the analysis as a set of key strategic issues.

There are several reasons for undertaking strategic analysis. One reason is to assess your organization's competitiveness, i.e., to determine its present competitive advantage. From this knowledge, strategy and future competitive advantage can be built. Another reason is to develop a list of key strategic issues faced by your organization or business unit. These issues are those that must be addressed through the ensuing strategic planning.

Step One

FORMING A PLANNING TEAM

Strategic analysis is generally too complex a task for an individual to undertake alone. Hence it is generally advisable to form a team.

Make implementation the first thought, not an afterthought.

In deciding on the composition of your planning team, there are a number of things to be considered: its size; the levels of the organization to be involved (for example, whether it will be only senior management); the functions to be represented (only line management? or staff too?); whether outsiders will be present (e.g., customers, suppliers or board members). Finally, the composition of the team must be such as to lead to ownership, commitment and implementation. (Appendix B, "Involving a Board in Strategic Planning," provides some guidelines for having a board play an effective role in the development of a strategic plan.)

The basic principle in structuring a planning team is to ensure that sufficient industry knowledge and experience are represented and that there is commitment to the strategic plan's implementation. (To dodge the pitfalls, see Chapter 11, "The Need for Action.") To carry out this principle, you must *think implementation first, not last*. The basic problem that most people experience in strategic analysis and planning is that they make implementation an afterthought, rather than the first thought. Once implementation comes first, the design and composition of the planning team take on totally different dimensions.

Step Two

PROFILING COMPETITORS

Once formed, your planning team needs to turn its attention to the remaining steps in the list above. The first of these is profiling competitors.

Most organizations do a relatively good job of monitoring customers and an extremely poor job of monitoring competitors. One reason for this is the lack of a structure that facilitates the tracking of competitor activity. Marketing and sales departments have as their specific responsibilities to ascertain and meet the needs of customers but, in most organizations, there is no department or individual whose specific purpose is to track the activities of competitors. This blind spot is a serious one that needs to be addressed.

Build up a picture of what your competitors are good — or bad — at.

Figure 4.1 is a modification of a figure previously encountered (3.1); here there is one important addition: competitors.

For each of the stereotypical key stakeholders — customers, suppliers, employees, owners — there exists a set of different competitors. Those for an organization's customers are different from those for owners. Different again are the competitors for employees, although these latter competitors may include those for customers.

If you are to develop effective strategy, it is essential that you have a complete understanding not only of your organization's key stakeholders, but also of the competitors for them. *Competitive advantage is doing something better than rivals, in the eyes of key stakeholders.* Thus, knowledge of what your competitors are capable of doing is vital.

Consequently, a profile of your organization's competitors must be developed. Take, for example, the competitors for your customers. A profile should be built around their management, their products and their likely future moves. Recent changes in their management or board structure and

Figure 4.1 **Strategy Development via Strategic Factors**

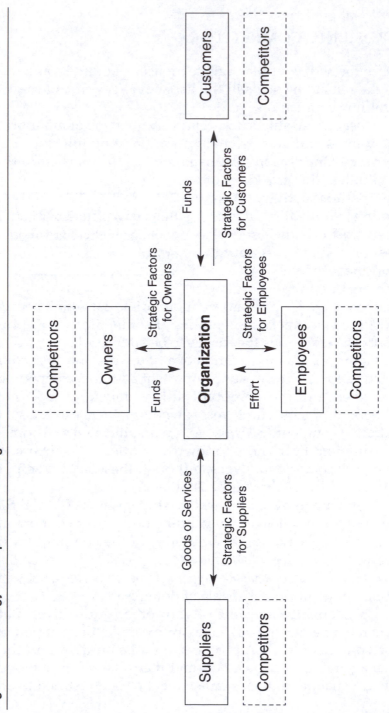

external pressures on performance should be documented as part of this profile. This helps you make deductions about competitors' likely future actions. It also assists in assessing competitors' performance.

The reason for profiling your competitors is that you intend to assess their performance versus yours on

> **Competitive advantage is doing something better than rivals, in the eyes of key stakeholders.**

strategic factors. In other words, as part of strategic analysis, you want to know which of you has the competitive advantage relevant to key stakeholders. Profiles of your competitors assist in undertaking a competitive assessment on strategic factors.

Step Three

IDENTIFYING STRATEGIC FACTORS

Besides understanding your competitors, you have to identify the strategic factors in your industry for each of your key stakeholders. We see this illustrated in the following case; while a real organization, its name has been changed.

MIDDLETON TIMBER

Middleton Timber is a subsidiary company of a larger public company. Middleton Timber manufactures trusses, frames and pre-hung doors, and supplies timber and ancillaries to builders and owner-builders. Trusses are those pre-manufactured components that hold up the roofs of houses, while frames are the prefabricated walls of houses. Among ancillaries are included fiber sheeting, particleboard flooring and timber moldings. The pre-hung door product was pioneered by Middleton Timber many years ago, and consists of a door already hung in its doorjamb, with the architrave attached.

As we noted, Middleton Timber's customers are builders

and owner-builders. The bulk of contract housing is controlled by about twenty builders. The major item purchased by Middleton Timber is radiata pine for the manufacture of the trusses and frames. Contracts are won in the industry through a process of quotation. A builder has a house design that it submits with a specification to a number of suppliers like Middleton Timber. Each supplier quotes a price based on the details submitted and wins the job (or not) on that basis. It is a process that results in intense rivalry.

Occupations represented at Middleton Timber include management, clerical staff, estimators, sales representatives, crane operators and factory employees who operate the saws and nail guns used in manufacture. The organization chart in Figure 4.2 displays the various positions.

Figure 4.2   Organization Chart of Middleton Timber

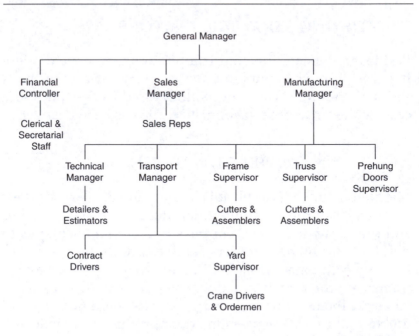

Four stakeholders were identified as having a major impact on the organization's prosperity. These key stakeholders and the relevant strategic factors are listed below:

Owners (holding company)
- Dividends
- Capital growth (shareholders' funds)
- Company reputation
- Operational performance

Customers (builders)
- Price and trade terms
- Product quality (consistency)
- Range of products
- Customer service
- Delivery

Suppliers (timber suppliers)
- Financial security of Middleton
- Consistency of orders
- Standardization of timber specification
- Order lead time
- Trade terms
- Size of orders

Employees
- Job security
- Job requirements
- Company reputation
- Physical working conditions
- Rewards
  - recognition
  - pay
  - training and development
  - bonus
  - promotional opportunities
- Co-worker relationships

(Note that in the case of suppliers, we are concerned here

with the performance of Middleton Timber with respect to suppliers, not with supplier performance.)

What this example illustrates is the importance of identifying an organization's key stakeholders which, in turn, affects the identification of strategic factors. If suppliers, for instance, had been omitted from the list, the strategic factors for suppliers would also have gone unnoted by Middleton Timber.

In addition to the collective experience of your planning team, there are other ways to uncover strategic factors. While the list below relates particularly to *customers*, a similar list could be drawn up for any key stakeholder of your organization or business unit.

- Customer responses to performance
  (e.g., letters, phone calls, conversations)

- Sales force feedback
  (e.g., sales reports on product/service sales)

- Customer surveys
  (e.g., questionnaire or interviews)

- Customer focus groups
  (i.e., small-group, in-depth discussions)

- Competitor activity
  (e.g., changes in their performance)

Customer Responses to Performance

Through letters, phone calls and conversations, your organization receives feedback from customers regarding their satisfaction or dissatisfaction with your performance.

A hotel, for example, may invite comments by leaving questionnaires in guests' rooms. Complaints aired via phone calls and conversations also indicate how customers evaluate the hotel's performance. These evaluations, if properly used, help the hotel identify the strategic factors for its guests. Strategic factors, you might recall, were in part defined as the decision criteria used by stakeholders to assess an organization's performance. By requesting feedback, the hotel is tapping into what the decision criteria (strategic factors) are. Regular feedback will also indicate how evaluations may change over time.

One organization in the frozen food industry has established a sophisticated customer complaints system for itself. This requires that each complaint be logged and examined for ideas in one of two categories. The first concerns process improvement. For example, if the complaint were about contaminants in the company's frozen peas, then the process by which these contaminants were included would be examined.

The other category of complaints concerns what we would call strategic factors. For example, if the complaint were that the packs of frozen peas were too large, then this could be the basis of a new product idea. Follow-up might show that the complaint came from people who live alone and do not require large packs of frozen peas. This could see the introduction of a smaller pack for these buyers. Here we have moved into the strategic factor, *range of products*.

Customer responses to your performance can be used creatively to assess the existence of strategic factors.

These examples illustrate how customer responses to your performance can be used creatively to assess the existence of strategic factors as well as any shifts in the importance that customers attach to those factors.

Sales Force Feedback

This next method involves the sales force deliberately seeking feedback from customers in order to identify strategic factors or pick up any shift in emphasis. This may occur via sales reports. If an organization is selling trusses and other building products to builders, for example, its sales force is in a position to pick up clues as to how builders make the decision to choose one supplier over another. But our methods can be more direct.

Suppose, in the case of Middleton Timber encountered earlier in this chapter, we wished to determine the strategic factors for customers (builders). One direct approach would be to visit them and ask, "The last time you chose to purchase from us instead of from the competition (or vice versa), how did you make that decision?" The answer would involve their decision criteria, the five strategic factors for customers of Middleton Timber: price and trade terms, product quality (consistency), range of products, customer service and delivery.

Customer Surveys

Surveying customers is a third way to identify strategic factors. A suitably designed questionnaire can elicit the criteria that are important to customers when they make up their minds which product or service to choose.

> You can get useful information on strategic factors simply by interviewing a small number of customers

Two types of customer surveys come to mind. One contains open-ended questions, from which are likely to emerge the strategic factors relevant to customer decision-making. Returning to the example of Middleton Timber, the customers (builders) could be sent or handed a questionnaire that included a question regarding their decision to purchase from Middleton Timber rather than one of its competitors. This question is similar to that used by the sales force on a face-to-face basis. We might ask: "How did you make the decision to purchase materials similar to those supplied by Middleton Timber?" If the questionnaire is properly administered, the answer should be similar to the one given to the sales force.

A second type of customer survey features closed questions that customers respond to on a scale, such as an importance scale. For example, the respondents may be given a number of decision criteria and asked to rate their importance in a decision to purchase timber products from Middleton Timber versus the competition. These could be the five strategic factors already identified: price and trade terms, product quality (consistency), range of products, customer service and delivery. Such a method could be useful in determining the relative importance of strategic factors to Middleton Timber's customers.

If you're like most people, the mention of customer surveys sends a shiver up your spine. What generally comes to mind is a large and expensive undertaking, with thousands of questionnaires being sent out and then processed for results, usually with the aid of a market research organization. We stress that this is not the type of survey envisaged here. You don't need thousands of questionnaires to identify how your customers make decisions. You're interested in the qualitative aspects of that process. You're interested in the decision criteria used. And you can get useful information on strategic factors simply by interviewing a small number of customers.

Let me give you an example that my company was involved in. The organization involved imported gift products, especially from Asian countries. Once they arrived, the products were distributed by the importer to retail stores. These stores were small gift shops, such as can be found in all our suburbs and large shopping malls. As part of a strategic planning exercise, the importer wished to identify the strategic factors relevant to its customers, i.e., the retail stores.

To do this, we conducted interviews of the owners of a sample of sixteen retail stores. One of the questions we asked was how they made their decision to purchase from the importer rather than from his competition, and vice versa. From the answers, a clear pattern emerged about halfway through the interviews. By the end of the tenth session, we could be eighty to ninety per cent sure that we had captured the strategic factors relevant to the retail stores. The remaining six interviews basically confirmed the results of the first ten.

This example illustrates what we are concerned with in determining strategic factors via customer "surveys." The emphasis is on quality, not quantity, and we're interested in decision criteria, not statistical analysis of vast quantities of data.

Customer Focus Groups

Customer focus groups are also effective in identifying strategic factors. These groups engage in discussions that range widely around a chosen topic. They can be held over dinner, for example, as the aim is usually to achieve informality. Under the guidance of a leader, the focus might be on how members of the group go about choosing a motor vehicle, for instance.

We can envisage such an in-depth discussion taking place with a group of customers of training organizations. The discussion would range freely over how these customers choose to attend the public seminars of one training organization over another and what determines these decisions. These, of course, are strategic factors.

Competitor Activity

The four previous methods for identifying strategic factors involve interacting with customers. We track their responses to our performance, we obtain feedback via our sales force, we survey our customers or we talk to them in a focus group. This next and final method involves keeping an eye on competitors.

A planning team may detect a marketplace change in strategic factors by observing changes in competitor activity. For example, if a competitor suddenly emphasizes product range as a competitive advantage, then perhaps he has picked up something in the marketplace that the team hasn't. The latter should re-examine the strategic factors it has previously identified and change them if necessary.

BRITISH AIRWAYS

Whilst still staying with Step 3, "Identifying Strategic Factors," let's now turn our attention to the approach of British Airways. This airline employs the first of the five previous methods to identify strategic factors and monitor its performance on them. In other words, it employs "customer responses to performance" to continually seek its customers' perspective on its service, taking their pulse, so to speak, in an area that might give it competitive advantage. It also employs "competitor activity," the fifth method for identifying strategic factors, to trace its competitors. It will match its competitors on strategic factors if there is a hint that competitors might be gaining an advantage.

The purpose of all this activity is to reflect the actual customer perspective on British Airways' performance, rather than the airline's perspective on its own performance. The company realizes that self-assessment can be both biased and self-justifying.

British Airways uses a number of performance measures of customer service. These include punctuality, aircraft cleanliness, time taken for a telephone customer to be put through to a reservations agent, check-in performance, satisfactory in-flight and ground services, and the number of involuntary downgrades in a given time period. Readings on such measures are taken monthly and reported monthly to the Chairman, the Managing Director, the Chief Financial Officer, and management responsible for service and performance.

British Airways also springs into action if a competitor introduces a new service or if collected data suggests that a problem or threat exists. But it recognizes the importance of not being misled. When a competitor offered a free limousine service to business-class and first-class passengers, British Airways was naturally tempted to follow suit. However, further research discovered that its passengers were unsure whether this service was really worthwhile. They appeared to prefer a place to relax and freshen up at the end of a long journey. Hence, it was these facilities that were established, in preference to the limousine service.

This example provides a snapshot of the way an organization like British Airways not only keeps in touch with its customers, but takes their view of its performance. It stands in their shoes, so to speak. It tries to identify the strategic factors relevant to them, from their perspective, and then it sets about monitoring its performance precisely on those factors.

You must assess your organization's performance from the outside in, not the inside out.

There may be a lesson in this for your organization, as in the past you may have been assessing performance by looking *inside out*, rather than *outside in*. In other words, you may have defined your performance on behalf of your key stakeholders from *your* perspective as an insider, rather than from their perspective as outsiders.

Step Four

COMPLETING A COMPETITIVE ASSESSMENT MATRIX

Let's think of a scenario that might occur within your organization or business unit. Suppose you have assembled your planning team and you wish to assess how well the organization or business unit and its competitors are doing. Specifically, you'd like to know how competitive your organization or unit is on strategic factors.

One way is by using what we call a *Competitive Assessment Matrix*. My company asks organizations to complete this matrix as part of undertaking strategic analysis. The task can be very illuminating in itself because, in many cases, organizations and business units do not have sufficient information to complete it fully. This fact alone is quite a discovery. What's also interesting is how differently members of a planning team rate their organization.

Figure 4.3 is a Competitive Assessment Matrix for the Middleton Timber Company. The five strategic factors relevant to the key stakeholder, *customers*, are used to assess Middleton Timber and its competitors (Hudsons, Longreach, Coussins and R.J. White in the table). An eleven-point rating scale has been used (shown at the bottom of the table). By employing this scale and a table such as this, your planning team can make an assessment of the performance of your organization or business unit relative to your competitors.

Remember that while this is an example of a competitive assessment on the strategic factors for *customers*, a similar matrix could be developed for suppliers, for owners, for employees and for any other key stakeholder.

Let's now look at the details in Figure 4.3. We see that Middleton Timber is about average on product quality, but is close to an exceptional performer on range of products; its range is very wide compared to that of its competitors. This fact may give Middleton Timber a strong competitive advantage, particularly when compared to R.J. White, whose range of products is narrow. We also note that Middleton Timber is average on delivery and just below average on customer service. On price, the company is close to "abysmal"! Relative to the competition, with the exception of Coussins, its prices are very high — hence the low rating. The leader on price is Hudsons, with its rating of "8," but this is that company's only distinguishing feature.

Each of the organizations has been characterized in the Figure's right-hand column. Middleton Timber has a large product range, but no distinguishing features on other strategic factors. Provided customers call for a wide range of products from a single supplier, it has a competitive advantage there. It certainly has no advantage on price. On product quality, delivery and customer service, it is about average. By contrast, Hudsons rates a mark of distinction on price (hence the title, "Price Cutter"), but it is average or below average on all the other strategic factors.

Longreach is average on all five strategic factors. As "Mr Average," with no observable competitive advantage, this

Figure 4.3 **Competitive Assessment Matrix**

Competitor	Strategic Factors					
	Product Quality	**Range of Products**	**Delivery**	**Customer Service**	**Price**	
Middleton Timber	5	9	5	4	2	Large product range, no other distinguishing features
Hudsons	2	5	5	2	8	"Price Cutter"
Longreach	5	5	5	5	5	"Mr Average"
Coussins	5	4	8	2	2	Great Delivery!
R.J. White	8	1	9	7	7	"Successful Niche Player"

Rating Scale

0	1	2	3	4	5	6	7	8	9	10
Abysmal Performer					Average Performer Compared to Competitors					Exceptional Performer

company would struggle to survive in the industry. Coussins, by contrast, excels on delivery, which is complete and on time in ninety-nine per cent of cases. This company is about average on product quality and range of products, but well below par on customer service and price. Is great delivery sufficient to give Coussins competitive advantage and significant market share? Time will tell.

Finally, we come to an interesting player in the market, R.J. White. The figures in Figure 4.3 tell us that this company is well above average on all factors except range of products. Indeed, it carries a very narrow product range. As the table suggests, it is a "Successful Niche Player." We see this trend emerging in many industries. On the one hand, Middleton Timber has positioned itself to cover almost every product that a builder may require but, in so doing, has sacrificed customer service and price. In contrast, R.J. White has decided to position itself strategically to cater for a narrow product range, letting the customer "shop around" for what it doesn't carry, while it excels on all the other four strategic factors. This can be a very successful strategy.

Implementing the Competitive Assessment Matrix

This tool can be very useful in seeing how your competitors have positioned themselves in your industry and, of course, it can be employed for any of your key stakeholders – not just customers. It helps an organization like Middleton Timber that is struggling to decide where it needs to concentrate its efforts. It also assists a planning team to see where competitive advantage can be created.

The way we have tackled the Competitive Assessment Matrix may tend to suggest that it is simple to use. While it is indeed a simple tool, it requires a considerable amount of information and knowledge from a planning team. So let's now review what you need in order to undertake it.

The first thing is knowledge of the competitors for your key stakeholders. You might recall that the second step in our list for analyzing strategic performance was profiling competitors. You can now see the importance of that step. In developing these profiles, you will build up a picture of what those competitors are good or bad at. However, the Competitive Assessment Matrix requires a planning team to go further.

"Going further" means identifying the strategic factors relevant to your organization or business unit and its competitors.

Now the hard work really begins. The next step for your planning team is to fill in the cells in the matrix for each competitor and for your own company/organization or business unit, using the 11-point scale. To be able to do this effectively, your team obviously has to have a good grasp of how your organization or business unit and its competitors are performing on strategic factors. Further, it needs to be taking each key stakeholder's perspective as it completes those ratings. There is no room for delusion or self-justification in this exercise.

It's been our experience that many organizations struggle to complete a Competitive Assessment Matrix satisfactorily.

It's been our experience that many organizations struggle to complete a Competitive Assessment Matrix satisfactorily. Often they're unsure of who their competitors really are. In addition, they may not have done the necessary research to be able confidently to list the strategic factors relevant to a key stakeholder, e.g. customers or employees. Further still, they struggle to make *informed* assessments of performance.

This lack of knowledge, these blind spots, these inabilities are in themselves instructive to a planning team. How can anyone develop effective strategy if current competitive advantage is not known? The answer is, of course, that it can't be done. So a planning team *must* do the necessary research in order to complete a Competitive Assessment Matrix in an informed way.

This lack of knowledge, these blind spots, these inabilities are in themselves instructive to a planning team.

Finally, if you do intend

to employ our Competitive Assessment Matrix in your organization or business unit, discourage guessing. When an informed assessment cannot be placed in a cell, please put a question mark. Guessing may be highly misleading, adversely affecting the strategy development that follows.

Step Five

DEVELOPING A COMPETITIVE ADVANTAGE PROFILE

The fifth step in analyzing strategic performance is completing what we call a *Competitive Advantage Profile* for each product or service, based on strategic factors.

The Competitive Assessment Matrix is an overall assessment. For instance, in the column for product quality in Figure 4.3, the numbers 5, 2, 5, 5, and 8 give a global assessment of Middleton Timber's performance against competitors. Two questions arise here:

1. In what detailed ways is Middleton Timber better than Hudsons and worse than R. J. White on product quality?

2. Is any particular product contributing to this score? For instance, is product quality high on trusses, but not on frames?

To tackle these and similar questions, use our Competitive Advantage Profile, by product or service. Before doing so, you need to —

- identify each of your major products or services;
- identify the market leader or nearest competitor for each.

The development of a Competitive Advantage Profile is illustrated below for Concord — a real organization, but not its real name.

CONCORD

Concord is an organization in the financial information industry. It provides information to stockbrokers and other organizations: stock prices, foreign exchange rates, etc.

The strategic factors relevant to Concord's customers are:

- Product functionality, content and timeliness
- Product reliability
- Customer after-sales service
- Pricing and contract flexibility.

Concord had already completed a Competitive Assessment Matrix and wished to compare its performance with its market leader or, if it is the market leader, its nearest competitor on its four major products. These are shown in Figure 4.4: money, news, equities and pagers. The table also lists the market leader or nearest competitor for each of these products. In the case of money and news, Concord itself is the market leader, and its nearest competitors are Kidder and Promax, respectively. In equities, Vasse is the market leader, while the market leader in pagers is Murray.

Figure 4.4   **Major Products Against Market Leader or Nearest Competitor**

Product	Market Leader or Nearest Competitor
Money	Nearest competitor: Kidder
News	Nearest competitor: Promax
Equities	Market leader: Vasse
Pagers	Market leader: Murray

The four strategic factors formed the basis for Concord's comparison with the others on each of its major products. The results for one of these products, *equities*, are shown in Figure 4.5, which lists the strategic factors and details the net advantages for Vasse, the market leader on sales, and for Concord.

Figure 4.5   Competitive Advantage Profile for Equities

Vasse

Net Advantages

**Product Functionality,
Content and Timeliness**
- Provides broker research
- Historical news
- Has entrenched customer base in institutional equities
- Can take other information feeds
- More extensive technical content and applications

Product Reliability
- Nil

Customer After-Sales Service
- Specialised staff
- Faster response time

Pricing and Contract Flexibility
- Nil

Concord

Net Advantages

**Product Functionality,
Content and Timeliness**
- Faster quotes access
- Easier to use
- Better domestic news coverage
- Better graphics
- Better money product
- Data control

Product Reliability
- Nil

Customer After-Sales Service
- Nil

Pricing and Contract Flexibility
- Nil

This Competitive Advantage Profile for *equities* tells us that on product reliability, as well as pricing and contract flexibility, Vasse has no net advantages over Concord. However, on product functionality, content and timeliness, as well as customer after-sales service, differences emerge. In the case of customer after-sales service, Concord has no net advantages, whereas Vasse has. Its customer after-sales service outscored that of Concord on the Competitive Assessment Matrix (not shown here).

The reasons for Vasse's superior performance are shown in this Competitive Advantage Profile: they have more specialized staff and a faster response time. Concord may wish to equal and then exceed Vasse's performance on this strategic factor in order to obtain competitive advantage.

The picture with product functionality, content and time-liness is mixed. While Vasse has clear advantages, so does Concord. As Vasse is the market leader on sales, it must be doing something right. Perhaps the advantages that it has are more in tune with what customers want than the advantages Concord offers. Clearly Concord needs to examine this question, because its answer could determine the direction of company strategy.

Implementing the Profile

The above example illustrates the use of the tool we have invented and called the Competitive Advantage Profile. It takes part of the Competitive Assessment Matrix and explodes it into detail, showing the features of performance on strategic factors that sit behind the assessments in the Matrix. One advantage of going into these details is that a planning team is thus better able to see avenues for developing strategy.

As was the case with the Competitive Assessment Matrix, the Competitive Advantage Profile does require a planning team to have considerable knowledge at its fingertips. Yet, not every team is clear at the outset about the market leader in its field or, if it is the market leader, its nearest competitor. Once these competitors are identified, their performance on strategic factors must be determined — in detail, as in Figure 4.5. The planning team needs to understand the causes of competitive advantage.

Step Six

SUMMARIZING RESULTS AS KEY STRATEGIC ISSUES

The final step involves summarizing the analysis of your organization's performance as a set of key strategic issues. *A key strategic issue is an item that will have a significant impact on the prosperity of an organization or business unit and which must be addressed via the strategic plan.*

We are not talking about operational issues here. There is a tendency for planning teams to gravitate towards the operational rather than the strategic. After all, operational issues occupy more than ninety per cent of every manager's day. They are uppermost in every manager's mind. It is only natural, therefore, that when planning teams sit down to consider "what needs to be done," they focus on the operational rather than the strategic.

Strategic issues have an outward focus and relate to "matters in the marketplace" of an organization or business unit. "Breadth versus depth in product lines" is an example of a strategic issue. Operational issues, by contrast, have an inward focus and are concerned with organizational structure, systems and processes. "Ineffective communication" is an example of an operational issue, even though it may eventually affect performance. (Appendix A, "Strategic Versus Operational Plans: Is There a Difference and Does it Matter?" talks about the difference between strategic and operational decisions and plans.)

The list of key strategic issues should number less than 10 and makes an easy-to-use checklist for planning activity. In one way or another, your strategic plan must reflect these issues.

Below are three sample lists of key strategic issues. We derived them by working with planning teams within each organization and by applying at least some of the steps for analyzing strategic performance outlined in this chapter. The organizations are real, but their names have been changed.

NORTHBRIDGE UNIVERSITY

There were 15 on the planning team in the case of Northbridge University, including the Vice Chancellor. Most of the other 14 people came from the faculties of the university, but included senior administrative staff. The university is composed of the Faculties of Business, Humanities and Social

Sciences, Law and Medicine, among others.

As a private university, there is major concern with funding and attracting local and overseas students. The university receives no government funds for teaching, so its strategic plan needed to focus on the university's funding over the next three years.

Among the key strategic issues identified by the planning team were:

- How to improve market perceptions of Northbridge University
- Value-added quality of graduates and differentiation of graduates
- Improving product and product delivery
- Greater emphasis on vocational and tertiary education in society
- How to compete with trend towards year-long education
- Globalisation of education
- Pricing of product

FARMER FINANCE

The role of Farmer Finance is to assist the rural sector with funding. It is government-owned and established many years ago to supplement the activities of banks in the private sector. Its aims include to promote the establishment, growth and stability of rural industry, to promote economic growth and to provide financial and other services in a profitable and competitive manner.

Farmer Finance's strategic planning team identified the following among the organization's key strategic issues:

- Strong competition in the marketplace for finance
- Falling commodity prices in agriculture
- World currency markets and their impact on farmers' incomes
- Competition from banks and other financial providers

- Further consolidation of farms and its impact on customer base
- Increased emphasis on environmental issues and sustainability in farming
- Negative attitude of farmers towards banking competitors

CONSULTING BUSINESS UNIT – ENVIRO ELECTRICITY

The Consulting Business Unit within Enviro Electricity is an example of a business unit within an organization that wishes to develop a strategic plan to assist in its competitiveness and future direction.

The Consulting Business Unit is located within an organization whose expertise is in the generation of hydroelectricity and it has managers for electrical and mechanical engineering, civil and water resources engineering and business and project services. It has a dual role. Within Enviro Electricity, it provides consulting services in job and project management, but it also sells its services outside the organization and internationally. Its strengths are that it has world-class skills and experience in hydropower and water resources management. There are many opportunities both nationally and internationally for applying those skills. Among the key strategic issues it identified for itself are the following:

- Need to clarify our business image
- Need to diversify customer base beyond its current limitations
- Strategic fit of Consulting Business Unit within Enviro Electricity
- Technological development in key competencies
- Structure of electricity industry

THE IMPORTANCE OF ANALYSIS

Much strategic planning is undertaken, unfortunately,

without appropriate analysis. In some cases, teams do no analysis at all. They simply develop strategy without taking the time to identify strategic factors — understandably, perhaps, since this concept is unknown to many.

Other planning teams do undertake analysis, but of the wrong type. They dive into spreadsheets of accounting results, analyze income statements and balance sheets, and get bogged down in finance and accounting — all without first getting a strategic perspective on the performance of their organization or business unit.

Because strategic factors have remained unidentified, organizations and business units have lacked the tools to undertake effective strategic analysis. That's why they fall back on accounting spreadsheets. This chapter has now rectified this situation by supplying a range of techniques based on strategic factors, that get planning teams to think strategically.

Without taking a strategic perspective on performance, a team is likely to become embroiled in operational issues, failing to see the strategic ones. But if you follow the steps outlined in this chapter, your strategic planning will be much more *strategic* than it has been in the past.

Much strategic planning is undertaken without appropriate analysis.

We turn in the next chapter to how to set objectives for your organization or business unit.

CHAPTER 5

WHERE ARE YOU GOING?

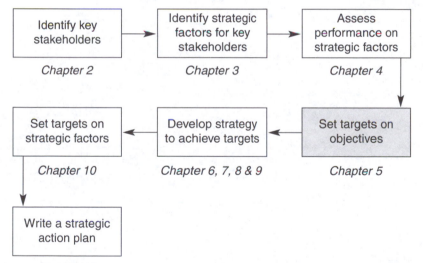

Identify key stakeholders	Identify strategic factors for key stakeholders	Assess performance on strategic factors
Chapter 2	*Chapter 3*	*Chapter 4*

Set targets on strategic factors	Develop strategy to achieve targets	Set targets on objectives
Chapter 10	*Chapter 6, 7, 8 & 9*	*Chapter 5*

Write a strategic action plan

Chapter 11

If you don't know where you're going, any road will get you there. If you don't know your objectives, any strategy will do. It's for this reason that objective setting is so important.

Our approach to objective setting is unique but very effective.

The conventional approach is to set objectives as a single block, not categorized by key stakeholders. And this conventional approach doesn't work.

It doesn't work because you need to write separate strategies for customers, for employees, for suppliers, for owners, and so on. How can a *link* be established between strategy for employees, for example, and results on a set of objectives, if that set isn't classified according to key stakeholder? The answer is it can't. Obtaining results on objectives via particular strategy becomes, in the conventional approach, a guess at best, but more likely a leap of faith. Not really very satisfactory!

In response to this nonsensical situation faced by most organizations, we developed a fresh approach in our Strategic Factor System, the essence of which is illustrated in Figure 5.1.

Figure 5.1   Strategic Factors and Objectives

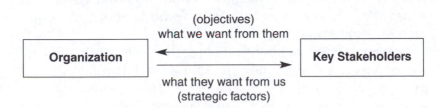

Figure 5.1 shows strategic factors as an outward flow from an organization (or business unit). We describe this as "what they (key stakeholders) want from us." We're familiar with this concept from Chapters 3 and 4 and especially Figure 4.1 on page 46.

What's new in Figure 5.1 is the idea that objectives are "what *we* want from *them*" (key stakeholders). But let me ask you a few questions. What do we want from customers? Isn't it money? What do we want from employees? Isn't it productivity and innovation? What do we want from our owners, be they shareholders or the government? Isn't it funds? And, what do we want from suppliers? Isn't it goods and services in full and on time? Shouldn't we be setting objectives in these areas?

If you don't know your objectives, any strategy will do.

We know your answer is "yes" because we've asked these questions of our clients many times. The answer is always "yes."

But as the conventional approach doesn't work, we're here to break the mold.

STRATEGY DEVELOPMENT FUNNEL

Before proceeding, look at Figure 5.2, because it gives an overview of where we've traveled up to this point and indicates what lies ahead.

We call the figure the "Strategy Development Funnel," as it starts with the broad questions about mission, vision and values and descends to specific questions about an action plan for individuals.

Mission is concerned with the question: what business are we in? Mission statements express the fundamental purpose of an organization or business unit. They are written for businesses, of course, but churches, hospitals, schools and charitable organizations also have to answer the question: what business are we in? It is a fundamental question and one that usually promotes considerable debate.

Vision, too, lies at the broad end of the Strategy Development Funnel. A vision statement is one that describes the mental picture held by an organization or business unit of what it will be like in some years' time. As the word implies,

Figure 5.2   **The Strategy Development Funnel**

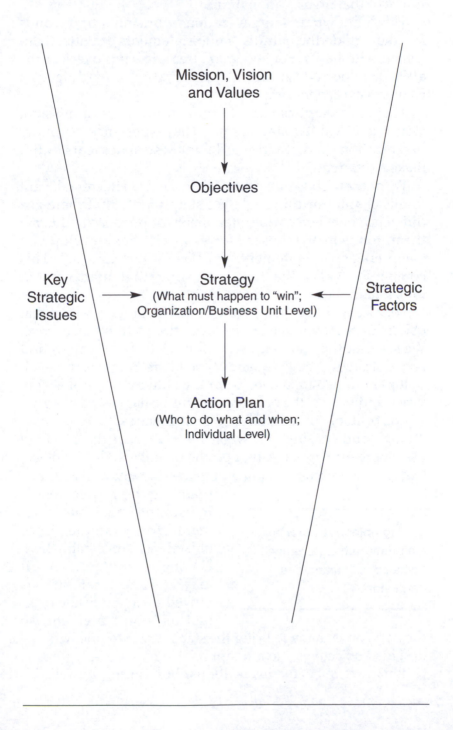

a vision statement is looking to the horizon and scoping the future of that organization or unit.

Values are what an organization or business unit stands for; they guide the culture. Value statements are often concerned with how an organization treats its employees or the attitude expected within the organization regarding, say, technical excellence or quality.

There are skeptics regarding the usefulness of mission, vision and values statements. The experience of many organizations is that writing down these statements didn't make a difference.

We don't wish to enter that debate here, as it isn't relevant to this chapter or this book. We simply note that there is a difference between *writing* statements of purpose and *living* them. Johnson & Johnson, for example, has developed a comprehensive statement entitled "Our Credo." This company "walks the talk," insisting that management understand the credo and live by it.

Let's leave that debate behind and look at the position that objectives occupy in the Strategy Development Funnel above. We see that they sit below mission, vision and values and above strategy. They are sandwiched here because, in developing them, we take cues from the statements of mission, vision and values; the objectives, in turn, shape the strategy.

You will, of course, realize that in practice, there is much "toing" and "froing" between the stages in the Strategy Development Funnel. Although the model shows that objectives follow mission, vision and values, it may well be that a planning team decides to revise the mission statement, for example, once objectives are established. Having set objectives, it may realize that it has moved away from the original mission statement, so the decision is made to bring the statement into line with the designed objectives. No attempt has been made in Figure 5.2 to illustrate such feedback loops, but these possibilities

Setting objectives can be a nightmarish experience because of "means/end" confusion.

should be kept in mind whenever the Strategic Development Funnel is encountered in this book.

MEANS-END SEQUENCE

If you've ever had the experience of sitting down with a planning team to develop objectives for a strategic plan, then you've probably had a nightmarish experience. Setting objectives without an effective framework is like asking the question: how long is a piece of string? Usually, in these sessions, you'll receive objectives that range from changing the carpet in the reception area to achieving a return on shareholders' funds. You feel they can't all be "right," but the statements all seem plausible. No one apparently disagrees, but everyone feels we're not getting anywhere. We're just "spinning our wheels."

What's going on here?

What's going on is the emergence of a means-ends sequence that exists in all organizations and business units. An example is shown in Figure 5.3. Via several other objectives, this example links the objective "to have good staff," to the objective "to show a return on investment."

Each objective is an end in itself, but also a means to an end. You can imagine a discussion regarding the establishment of objectives such as these. Someone might suggest that the objective is to have good staff. Who could disagree? Yet it could be stated that, rather than an end in itself, this objective is a means to an end, the end being to deliver effective customer service. Again, who could disagree with this statement? Except that it could be pointed out that delivering effective customer service is not an end, but a means to having satisfied customers. And so the discussion would continue, as one apparent end becomes a means to yet another end.

In a means-end sequence, the objectives are usually moving between different key stakeholders, as Figure 5.3 clearly indicates. The first means-end — to have good staff — relates to the key stakeholder, "employees." The second,

Figure 5.3 **Means-end Sequence**

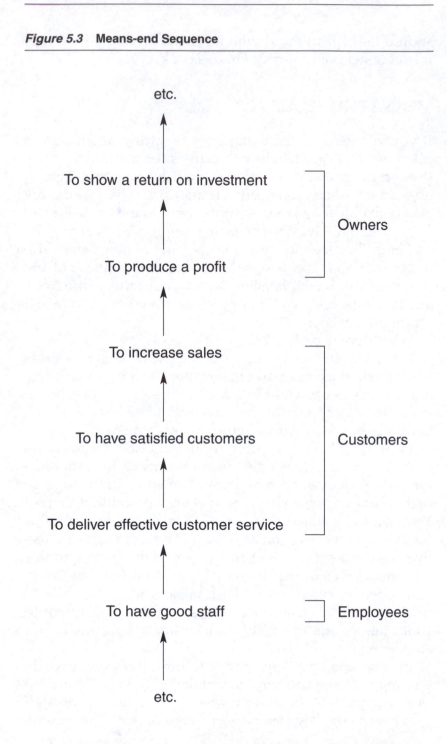

third and fourth means-ends are concerned with customers: effective customer service, satisfied customers and increased sales. The next two, to produce a profit and show a return on

> **In a means-end sequence, the objectives are usually moving between different key stakeholders.**

investment, relate to another group of key stakeholders, the owners. In short, Figure 5.3 is a mish-mash of objectives aligned with different key stakeholders.

Setting objectives and establishing targets is an important task in strategic planning. Without clear objectives, how does a planning team select a strategy from a range of options? And how would it know when the plan has achieved its target?

This chapter presents a breakthrough approach that our company has developed. It involves setting objectives by key stakeholder.

OBJECTIVES BY KEY STAKEHOLDER

The first point of departure from the conventional approach to objective setting is that we set objectives by key stakeholder. What this means is that objectives are developed, not as a single group for an organization or business unit (the conventional approach), but by key stakeholder. Objectives for cus-

> **Set objectives by key stakeholder — a very different approach.**

tomers, objectives for employees, objectives for suppliers, objectives for owners, objectives for any other relevant key stakeholder. This point of departure also establishes a position of clarity: the process is much clearer than when objectives are established as an undifferentiated set.

If key stakeholders are implicit in objective setting, then by making them *explicit*, objective setting should become easier. In fact it does.

Figure 5.4 has been encountered earlier in this book as Figure 4.1. The difference between this version and the previous one is that the word *objectives* has been introduced. In the previous version "funds" was present where the word "objectives" now sits (in the case of customers). The same goes for owners. In the case of employees, the word "effort" has been replaced by "objectives," while for suppliers, "objectives" has replaced the words "goods or services." In this section we explain what this substitution means.

Strategic factors for each of the key stakeholders are shown as outward flows from the organization. These are the things that an organization needs to get right as far as the key stakeholders are concerned. In the case of customers, as we know, strategic factors might be product quality, customer service, delivery and price.

But while an organization needs to build strategy around these factors, it also needs to identify what it *wants* from its key stakeholders. Otherwise, strategic planning could become a one-way street, with an organization giving all and getting little back. Figure 5.4 shows that what an organization gets back is results on its *objectives*.

In the case of customers, it wants funds, so objectives are based on this requirement. While organizations preach customer service and satisfaction, at the end of the day they want their customers' money. If, as in the case of a public library, the service is free, the library still wants something from its customers: goodwill, because this goodwill may lead to an increase in funds from the library's owner, the government.

In the case of suppliers, an organization or business unit wants the supply of goods or services, in full and on time. Objectives are set around this requirement. In the case of employees, an organization or business unit wants effort and again, objectives are based on this requirement. So the organization or business unit will do its darnedest on the strategic factors for employees, expecting the latter, in turn, to meet its objectives. Finally, an organization will apply itself to the strategic factors for owners to ensure that the owners continue to provide funds.

Figure 5.4 **Objectives and Strategic Factors**

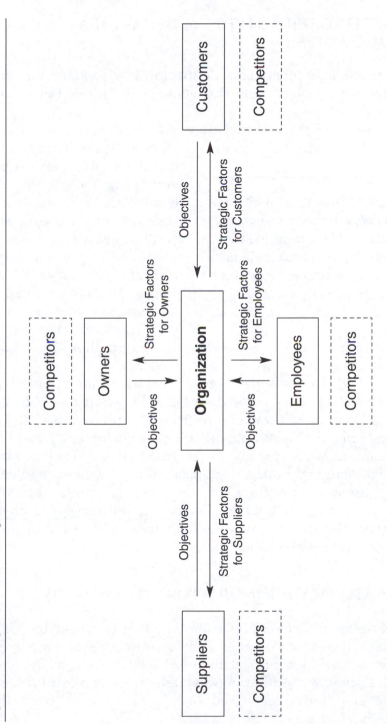

SETTING OBJECTIVES VIA BEHAVIORAL OUTCOMES

There's a step between identifying key stakeholders and developing objectives. This is the establishment of behavioral outcomes.

Behavioral outcomes are what we want our key stakeholders to do. Ask a planning team what are its organization's objectives, and you'll get blank looks. Ask the team what it wants its key stakeholders to do, and you'll get lively discussion.

> **Ask a planning team what are its organization's objectives, and you'll get blank looks. Ask the team what it wants its key stakeholders to do, and you'll get lively discussion.**

Figure 5.5 presents some typical behavioral outcomes. This is by no means a complete picture, nor can you transpose behavioral outcomes from one organization to another. They vary according to organization and industry.

What you can see in Figure 5.5 is the commonsense way in which we write down these behavioral outcomes. You can also see how they are translated into objectives. For example, the behavioral outcome for customers, "they buy more," is translated into "to increase sales." "They buy our high-margin products" is translated into "to increase sales of high-margin products." Remember, of course, that this Figure shows only *typical* behavioral outcomes and objectives. The appropriate ones for your organization or business unit may be quite different.

PERFORMANCE INDICATORS ON OBJECTIVES

If we're going to establish strategy that is framed by objectives, the objectives need to be quantified. Many organizations develop vague statements of "objectives" that are often described as "motherhood statements" or platitudes. We develop measures based on objectives and, from this

Figure 5.5   **Behavioral Outcomes and Objectives**

Typical Behavioral Outcomes	Examples of Objectives

• **Customers**
  – they buy more
  – they buy our high margin
    products
	• to increase sales
	• to increase sales of high
	  margin products

• **Suppliers**
  – they supply in full and on time
 	
  – they meet specifications
	• to increase orders received in
	  full and on time
	• to increase orders received that
	  meet specifications

• **Employees**
  – they stay
  – they attend
  – they work hard
  – they innovate
	• to decrease employee turnover
	• to decrease absenteeism
	• to increase productivity
	• to increase innovation

• **Owners** – they supply funds	• to maintain funds supplied

working list of measures, distil a short list called key performance indicators (KPI's).

How to translate objectives into key performance indicators is illustrated by the example of Suncoast Cancer
Council. We worked with this organization (not its real
name), assisting it to identify its key stakeholders, set objectives and develop KPI's on those objectives.

SUNCOAST CANCER COUNCIL

Suncoast Cancer Council was established by the government to promote cancer care in the community. It promotes
cancer prevention, sells cancer prevention products through
its thirteen retail stores, collects information on cancer cases
and fatalities, and reports this data to the government.

Suncoast Cancer Council has a wide variety of key stakeholders, including:

- Government as client
- Supporters
- Volunteers

For each of these key stakeholders, the Council established behavioral outcomes, a sample of which is shown in Figure 5.6. One of the outcomes was for the government to provide grants and contracts. In the case of supporters, one of the behavioral outcomes was to provide funds. With volunteers, one of the outcomes was to provide their time.

Figure 5.6 **Measuring Objectives for Suncoast Cancer Council**

Key Stakeholder	Behavioral Outcome	Objectives	KPI's for Objectives
Government as client	Provide grants and contracts	To increase funds from government via grants and contracts	• $ government grants and contracts
Supporters	Provide funds	To increase funds from supporters	• $ revenue – donors – supporters other than donors
Volunteers	Provide their time	To increase volunteer time	• # hours provided by volunteers

Figure 5.6 shows how each behavioral outcome has been converted into an objective. For example, the behavioral outcome for government as client, "provide grants and contracts," has been converted into the objective, "to increase funds from government via grants and contracts."

It's important to realize that objectives don't have to be in dollar terms. As we see in the case of volunteers, the behavioral outcome, "provide their time," has been converted into the objective, "to increase volunteer time."

Once you approach developing objectives in this way, measures emerge

It's important to realize that objectives don't have to be in dollar terms — but they must be quantified.

almost automatically. In Figure 5.6 you can see the shortlist of measures for objectives. We call these KPI's.

This example illustrates how we develop *quantified* objectives via our System. The first step is to identify key stakeholders. The second step is to write down the behavioral outcomes required from them. The third step is to convert those behavioral outcomes into objectives, and the last step is to develop measures, the shortlist of which constitutes the KPI's for those objectives.

Of course, in undertaking these steps, you must be selective about whom you nominate as key stakeholders and about the behavioral outcomes you list. Select only the important ones. If you are selective at this point, you will end up with a short list of objectives and key performance indicators. This helps to achieve focus in strategy development and, as a consequence, implementation effort.

ESTABLISHING TARGETS ON OBJECTIVES

The extent to which objectives influence strategy depends on the specific targets established for those objectives. In the case of Suncoast Cancer Council, if the target over the next three years were to maintain the existing level of government grants and contracts, a certain strategy would be developed to achieve this. If, on the other hand, the target were to double the dollars received, then an entirely different strategy would be designed.

Though not shown, you can imagine an additional column in Figure 5.6. It would be to the right of the "KPI's for Objectives" column, and its heading would be, "Targets." These would be targets on the KPI's for objectives which, in turn, are targets on the objectives themselves. For example, a target on "# hours provided by volunteers" could be "5,000 hours."

Much target setting is a haphazard affair. They are set, for example, on customer satisfaction, without reference to their effect on revenue, and vice versa. Hence, an organization may set the targets to raise revenue by ten per cent and customer satisfaction by five per cent, but not establish a cause-and-effect relationship between them. Of course, this should and must be done.

Key stakeholders have an impact on each other. Your employees, for example, are the drivers of the whole system, and their efforts influence results on objectives for all other key stakeholders. In setting targets for owners, then, you are able to identify the targets necessary for suppliers, customers and employees. Chapter 10 demonstrates this in more detail.

STREAMLINING OBJECTIVE SETTING

Planning teams have the potential to produce a vast array of statements that lead an organization or business unit nowhere, often being nothing more than platitudes or statements of the obvious. While no one may disagree with them, they usually do not advance an organization or business unit very far.

We have seen clients' obvious delight in being able to undertake objective setting with clarity.

This chapter has provided a significant advancement. The first of its components is that objectives are established *by key stakeholder.* This is a real breakthrough in objective setting. The second component is that for each key stakeholder we write behavioral outcomes, i.e., what an organization or business unit wants from them.

The third element is converting these behavioral outcomes into objectives, and the fourth is converting each objective into one or more key performance indicators (KPI's) via a set of measures. Establishing targets on these KPI's which, in turn, are targets on the objectives themselves, is the final ingredient. We believe this is a far better way to set objectives, and we feel confident about this affirmation because we have used the method with clients and seen their obvious delight at being able to undertake objective setting with clarity.

Our company, Strategic Factors, has developed *software* that assists in the steps described above. This software helps you capture key stakeholders, behavioral outcomes and objectives, as well as the measures appropriate to those objectives. These latter go into what we call a Measures Matrix. The short list of them goes into what we call a Focused Scorecard. If you want to link the Scorecards of several business units throughout your organization, our other package provides a major breakthrough here. Information on these products is available through our website *www.strategicfactors.com*

To achieve results on objectives, you need competitive advantage. It's to this topic we turn in the next chapter.

C H A P T E R 6

THE FATAL FLAW

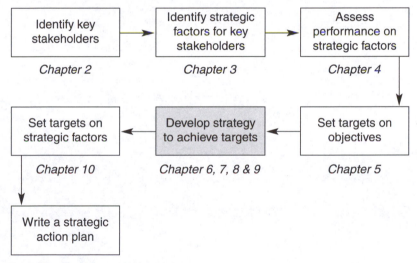

Identify key stakeholders	Identify strategic factors for key stakeholders	Assess performance on strategic factors
Chapter 2	*Chapter 3*	*Chapter 4*

Set targets on strategic factors	Develop strategy to achieve targets	Set targets on objectives
Chapter 10	*Chapter 6, 7, 8 & 9*	*Chapter 5*

Write a strategic action plan
Chapter 11

The fatal flaw in many organizations' strategies lies in their misunderstanding of competitive advantage — and this error *is* widespread.

Most organizations misread performance on internal processes and capabilities as competitive advantage. They become complacent in the knowledge that their systems are "best practice" or "quality." Yet the response to such claims should be, "So what?"

At which point the blood may drain from managers' faces.

In previous chapters we've explained how internal processes are mistaken for strategic factors. Unfortunately they are also mistaken for competitive advantage. This chapter demonstrates the development of strategy to achieve objectives, covering essential concepts such as value, differentiation and positioning.

RANGE OF COMPETITORS

Our definition of competitors may be broader than you have been used to in the past. You may have thought of competitors as relevant *only* to the relationship between an organization or business unit and its customers. The strategy literature emphasizes this almost to the exclusion of relationships between an organization and its other key stakeholders. Under this "customers only" perspective, the only competitors of British Airways, for example, are other airlines, such as Singapore Airlines, Japan Airlines and Qantas.

But the reality is that British Airways faces a much larger array of competitors through its transactions with key stakeholders *other than* customers. Take

Take a much wider view on who your competitors are.

the case of employees: not only are the airlines included, but also organizations outside the airline industry such as hotels and restaurants, and a vast array of other organizations competing for office staff. A different set of competitors also emerges for British Airways' suppliers and for its owners.

It may seem novel to suggest that an organization has competitors for its owners. This is not the way in which the term "competitors" is conventionally employed. However, competitors *do* exist for an organization's owners — whether they be shareholders of a public or private company, or the government, in the case of a public sector organization. Owners are one of the suppliers of funds and they can decide to put their money elsewhere.

In the case of British Airways, the competitors for its owners are, of course, other publicly listed airlines, but also any publicly listed organization that can show a better return than British Airways.

This wider view of competitors has been illustrated in Figure 4.1 on page 46 in Chapter 4, but the emphasis there was on key stakeholders and strategic factors. Here our emphasis is on competitors. They exist for *all* key stakeholders.

Public and Private Sector Differences

Whereas it is obvious that the shareholders of a public company, such as IBM, have many choices, many people do not realize that the "shareholders" of an organization such as the Department of Social Security (i.e., the government) also have many choices: the funds can be directed to defense, to education, to roads and bridges, etc.

This highlights one of the major differences between public and private sector organizations, as illustrated in Figure 6.1. In the case of the private sector, capital funds flow from the owners to the organization whereas, by and large, operating funds come from customers. In a public sector organization — one where there is no charge for services, such as education and social security — both capital and operating funds flow from the owners of the organization (i.e. the government).

Such public sector organizations maintain, should you ask them, that they do *not* have competitors. Social Security may say, for example, that it has none since no one else provides social security. However, when such an organization considers competitors in the wider context proposed here, it becomes obvious that it does have major competitors, on the

Figure 6.1 **Funds Flow in the Private and Public Sectors**

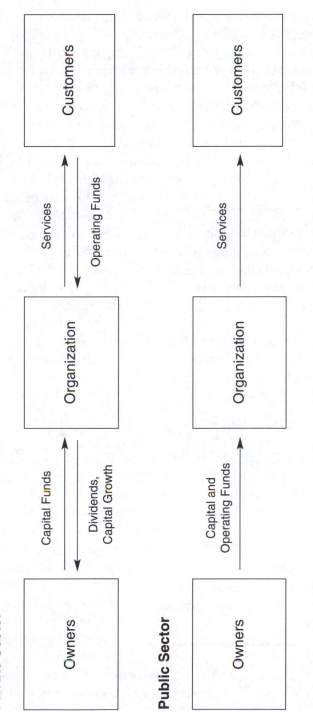

Private Sector

Owners — Capital Funds → Organization

Organization — Dividends, Capital Growth → Owners

Organization — Services → Customers

Customers — Operating Funds → Organization

Public Sector

Owners — Capital and Operating Funds → Organization

Organization — Services → Customers

owner's side at least. Defense and education are just two of the competitors for the funds that flow to social security. As illustrated in Figure 6.1, both capital and operating funds come from the owners of Social Security, and competition is indeed intense for that money.

It's important for you to define competitors as a much larger set than one that focuses only on your customers. Let me emphasize the point again: your organization or business unit faces competitors for *all* its key stakeholders. Don't be blinded by much of the strategy literature that focuses only on competitors for customers. Through our Strategic Factor System, you will begin to consider competitors as a much more diverse set of organizations than you have previously thought.

> **It's important to define competitors as a much larger set than one that focuses only on your customers.**

As value is what our key stakeholders seek from us and our competitors, we move on now to consider strategies to provide value superior to our competitors.

DEFINING VALUE

In strategic planning, the term "value" has been used in a number of different ways. In the case of economic value added, we are talking of operating profit minus taxes, minus cost of capital. If the value added is positive, an organization has performed effectively; the higher the value added, the more effective the performance — at least in terms of the definition.

> **It is the key stakeholders that make the assessment of value, not the organization itself.**

Proposed here is a different view of value: value based on strategic factors. Value is concerned with assessing the transactions (or potential transactions) between key stakeholders and the organization or business unit. In addition, it is the *key stakeholders that make the assessment* of value, not the organization itself. In the case of owners, for example, their perception of value relates to whether or not they are "getting a good deal" from their relationship with this organization. Likewise, other key stakeholders judge value on whether the transactions in which they are engaged with an organization are favorable to them.

One way of expressing value is "what we get for what we give." You will recall that we identified six strategic factors for one of 7-Eleven's key stakeholders, its customers:

- Location
- Hours of operation
- Customer service
- Range of goods sold
- Store presentation
- Price

The store offers (gives) location, hours of operation, customer service, range of goods sold and store presentation, while it expects (gets) payment. From a customer's point of view, the transaction looks like Figure 6.2.

Value from a customer's perspective is the balance between price, as an indicator of dollars spent (or to be spent), and the five other strategic factors. The charge for a bundle of items is weighed up against performance on the other five factors. If the equation is positive, such that customers feel they are getting a "good deal," they remain loyal. If, on the other hand, they don't think performance on these five factors is at least equal to the price, they look elsewhere.

What strategic factors serve to emphasize is how purely subjective value really is.

What strategic factors serve to emphasize is how purely subjective value really is.

Here we are talking about a *current* rather than a *potential* customer of a convenience store. But potential customers make similar calculations when they decide whether to become customers or not.

Figure 6.2   **Strategic Factors and Value – For Customers of 7-Eleven**

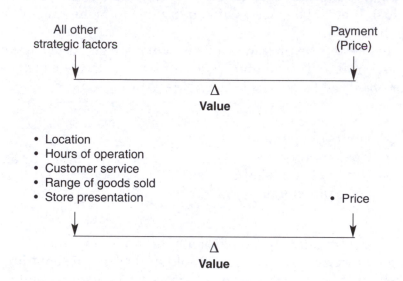

CHANCE LOTTERIES

Chance Lotteries (not its real name) is a government-owned entity that operates as a public sector corporation. Its products are lottery tickets that are bought through retail stores acting as agents. As a public sector corporation, it pays an annual dividend to its owner, the government. As a government corporation, it runs very much like a private sector organization, but it does have, as one would expect, some unusual reporting relationships to the government. Unlike an entity in the private sector, it is also subject to political influence.

The lotteries' five divisions are responsible for marketing, sales support, information technology services, finance and corporate services.

It's conventional to think of value in relation to customers. Yet *all* key stakeholders assess the value of their relationship with an organization or business unit. For employees of Chance Lotteries, for instance, the relevant strategic factors were:

- Remuneration
- Job challenge and security
- Equity
- Corporate culture
- Career prospects
- Location
- Job requirements

These factors — and they will vary, of course, depending on the organization, its employees and its industry — can be rearranged in value terms, as shown below. As far as the Lotteries employees are concerned, what they "get" is shown in the left column, while what they "give" is shown on the right.

• Remuneration	• Job requirements
• Job security	
• Equity	
• Corporate culture	
• Career prospects	
• Location	

In deciding whether to stay or leave, *current* employees weigh up remuneration, job security, equity, corporate culture, career prospects and location against job requirements, which indicate the effort required to do the work. Just as price was an indicator of the amount of funds required of a convenience store customer, job requirements indicate the amount of effort demanded of employees of Chance Lotteries.

For *potential* employees, the seven strategic factors are

also relevant in deciding whether or not they will join the organization at all. They are, in this way, like customers of a convenience store: they can "shop" somewhere else. A decision to join the lotteries organization will depend on their perception of value as indicated by balancing job requirements against the other six strategic factors.

STRATEGIC FACTORS, PERFORMANCE AND VALUE

The relationship between strategic factors and value is illustrated in Figure 6.3. It shows that strategic factors give rise to *decision criteria*. Key stakeholders use these criteria to make a decision to support one organization or business unit over another. For example, in the case of Chance Lotteries, these are the criteria used by potential employees to decide whether or not to become actual employees. Current employees also use these criteria to decide whether or not they should stay on.

Figure 6.3   **Strategic Factors and Value**

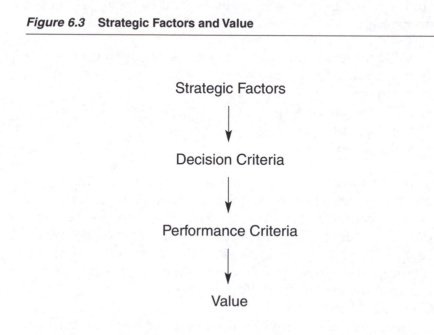

Once we become aware of strategic factors, we can see them everywhere. In deciding whether or not to quit jobs, it has been suggested that employees check these 10 warning signs:

- You have stopped learning and you're bored
- No feedback
- No ascent up the ladder
- You work in a toxic environment
- You have no life outside of work
- You simply don't care any more
- You feel regularly stressed, fatigued or ill
- You are losing confidence and credibility
- You're underpaid
- You're at odds with the company[1]

We can see from this list how these decision criteria are a different way of describing many of the strategic factors listed for employees of Chance Lotteries.

We can also look at strategic factors as *performance criteria*. The criteria used in the case of shareholders — dividends, capital growth, company reputation and operational performance — are the basis on which a current or potential shareholder evaluates a company's performance. If this performance is satisfactory, the present shareholder keeps his funds with the company. Should the performance on these four strategic factors drop below expectations, however, he or she will cease to invest there. And if a potential shareholder perceives performance as satisfactory, he or she will start investing in that company.

Once you become aware of strategic factors, you see them everywhere.

Figure 6.3 also links strategic factors to the perception of *value*. If the evaluation in relation to a certain company is positive, more positive than in the case of a competitor, then the customer will remain with that company. A similar situation holds for any set of key stakeholders. Owners balance the funds they provided against dividends and capital growth, as well as other strategic factors. Employees balance job requirements and strategic factors such as remuneration and career prospects.

Having a competitive advantage is not the same as having better technology or better systems.

To reiterate, value in our System is approached from key stakeholders' perspectives, not those of the organization or business unit. Looking at value in this way allows you to clearly articulate your competitive advantage.

STRATEGIC FACTORS AND COMPETITIVE ADVANTAGE

As we have said, value is the result of balancing strategic factors. *Competitive advantage is the extent to which an organization delivers value superior to that of its competitors.* This way of defining competitive advantage applies to the relationship between an organization or business unit and each of its key stakeholders.

Competitive advantage is the extent to which an organization delivers value superior to that of its competitors.

Let's return to the 7-Eleven convenience store example. As you will recall, the strategic factors for a convenience store were: location, hours of operation, customer service, range of goods sold, store presentation, price.

Let's now look at several ways in which a 7-Eleven store might achieve competitive advantage by producing superior value:

- The store might beat competitors on *location* if it were centrally located and not on a busy road, so as to be deemed more convenient. All other things being equal, in the eyes of current and potential customers, it would have produced value superior to its competitors.

- The store could rate higher than its competitors on *hours of operation*, staying open 24 hours a day, as contrasted to its competitors' 8-hour day. Again, all other things being equal, it would have produced superior value over its competitors.

- 7-Eleven's performance could be better than its competitors on *customer service*, with more polite and better-informed staff. This, once again, translates into superior value.

- Suppose our store sells a greater, yet more targeted, range of goods than its competition. It would thereby have, all other things being equal, a competitive advantage on the *range of goods sold.* In the eyes of current and potential customers, it has produced superior value over its competitors.

- If our store has a better layout, it would have a competitive advantage on *store presentation*, and its current and potential customers could view this as superior value.

- Finally, the store could be out in front because of its *prices*, if they are consistently lower than those of competitors. In the eyes of current and potential customers, its value would be superior to what its competitors are offering. Naturally, all other things would have to be equal, as in the above cases.

A combination of two or more factors could produce the same effect of superior value.

The example of a 7-Eleven store is used because it is one we can all appreciate. Who among us hasn't used the strategic factors listed above, in one way or another, to decide to buy from a particular store instead of its competitors?

Of course, life isn't as simple as the six individual descriptions above. Convenience stores generally don't stand out on only one strategic factor, such as location or customer service. In actual fact, the store we pick probably does slightly better on a couple of factors which, when taken together and put alongside our expectations, make us decide to buy from it rather than from the competition. Nonetheless, the individual descriptions above illustrate the principle that strategic factors not only underpin value, but are the drivers of competitive advantage.

Let's now turn our attention to a much larger food retailer, one that bases its strategy on strategic factors.

WOOLWORTHS AUSTRALIA

Woolworths Australia is a significant organization globally. It's ranked 415th in *Fortune's* 500 largest corporations in the world, with revenues of $11.9 billion and profits of $162 million. In *Fortune's* Food and Drug Stores Category, there are 25 companies worldwide out of the top 500. Woolworths ranks 22nd on profit, but 10th on profit as a percentage of assets.

Unrelated to the American Woolworths, but with a strong similarity to the U.S. Safeways, Woolworths Australia has guided its development by a keen focus on strategic factors.

Not long ago, the giant retailer spotted a significant new concern among its customers that caused a fundamental shift in its strategy: safety had become the dominant issue in shoppers' minds. The company's research found that a decade before, the principal reason people chose to shop in a given store was price — they looked to see what they could save. About five years ago, the emphasis moved from price to convenience. Location, another strategic factor, dominated. Customers wanted available parking, they wanted the stores to be close to home and close to other stores serving their needs. They also wanted longer hours.

Safety has become the dominant issue at present through a combination of causes. One of these was a disturbing incident: a producer of preserved meats distributed product that led to food poisoning and fatalities. This frightened a number of Woolworths' customers; they became concerned about the food they were purchasing from Woolworths and other stores. This concern has now been transformed by the debate about genetically modified food. Customers are seeking reassurance that the food they are buying, whether genetically modified or not, is safe to eat.

But Woolworths has ascertained that, in addition to purity of food, its customers are also concerned about physical safety in shopping centers.

Woolworths' strategy is clearly focused on strategic factors, four in particular: safety, price, location and hours of operation. Note also how the emphasis on strategic factors by a key stakeholder can shift over time. Safety is now relevant, whereas it wasn't earlier.

Of course, Woolworths is not without its competitors. Franklins, one of its major competitors, has changed its strategy, too. This followed a fall in Franklins' share of the national grocery market, from 16.2% to 14.3%. Woolworths holds 34.3%.

Franklins needed to fight back to regain its market share. Increasing the range of goods sold was the way taken. They felt they needed to move from a straight grocery-only store to a full-line supermarket retailer. They found that their customers had changed, wanting more convenience and wanting to be able to get everything from the one place. As Franklins saw it, price was still important, but so were other strategic factors like location, range and trading hours.

Of course, still other factors were involved, factors that retailers know also lead to success: image/brand values, store presentation and, of course, customer service.

What's illustrated in this example is how strategic factors underpin strategy and give rise to competitive advantage. Woolworths and Franklins are like two gladiators in the Colosseum, each having chosen its preferred weapons from among the strategic factors. Woolworths emphasizes safety and fresh food. Franklins emphasizes the range of goods it sells.

Franklins, however, is in catch-up mode, as Woolworths dominates the marketplace. Franklins has lost market share. What does it do to get it back? What does it do to grow to the size of Woolworths?

The answer lies in developing competitive advantage which, as we now appreciate, means delivering superior value on strategic factors.

WHAT COMPETITIVE ADVANTAGE IS NOT

When we view competitive advantage in the way outlined in this book, we bring our thinking back to the realities of the transactions between an organization or business unit and its key stakeholders. *Competitive advantage is doing something better than a competitor, but in a way valued by stakeholders.* The last phrase is an important rider here. What's important is not what we as members of an organization or business unit consider competitive advantage to be. It's how our key stakeholders define it. *That* is fundamental. We can delude ourselves that we have competitive advantage when, in actual fact, we don't.

Competitive advantage is not the same as having superior internal capabilities. Planning teams will often say that they have a competitive advantage because they have better technology, or more highly qualified employees, or a lower cost structure.

Competitive advantage is doing something better than a competitor, but in a way valued by stakeholders.

These capabilities may be the springboard to deliver competitive advantage, but managers should not be misled into thinking that they constitute competitive advantage itself. This important message is emphasized here.

These things mean nothing to customers or any other stakeholders unless they translate into something that *is* valued. For example, better information technology only means something to customers if it delivers better customer service, or if it allows an organization to achieve a lower price. It may be that the presence of more highly trained and skilled employees leads to better customer service but, if it doesn't, it is of no consequence as far as customers are concerned. It also means nothing in terms of competitive advantage.

Again, to be the lowest-cost producer in an industry is not a competitive advantage. Customers do not buy our costs, they pay our price. Being a low-cost producer is, of course, a desirable position to occupy in any industry but, unless this is translated into something customers or other stakeholders value (e.g., price in the case of customers), it means little in competitive advantage terms.

> **We're talking about a totally different way of looking at competitive advantage.**

We are not simply playing with words here. We're talking about a totally different way of looking at competitive advantage.

Many people view competitive advantage from an *inside-out* view. They look out at it from a vantage point inside their organization or business unit. What they see is what they do well and they tell themselves: "We have better technology; we have highly qualified employees; we have a low-cost structure." But this is an inside-out view of performance and competitive advantage. It is also the wrong view, as it misleads an organization or business unit into thinking it is doing well when, in reality, it may not be. Money is spent on such things as technology and the boast is made that a competitive advantage had been gained. This is, of course, nonsense, and it's one of the reasons many lean, mean, small organizations make major inroads into the market share of large and cumbersome ones.

To truly understand competitive advantage, we have to take an *outside-in* view: we must stand in the shoes of our key stakeholders, outside the organization looking in, not inside the organization looking out. When we take this stance, we get an entirely different picture and come to very different conclusions. Many organizations will see misspent dollars — dollars spent on technology in the vain hope of grabbing competitive advantage, dollars spent on training employees with courses they will never use to improve customer service. And so the list goes on.

Remember that competitive advantage is *how your key stakeholders perceive your performance on strategic factors*, not how you perceive your performance on internal processes, practices, systems and the like.

In the rest of this chapter, we deal with two important and useful concepts in strategy: differentiation and positioning, and how they, too, are underpinned by strategic factors. A number of examples will illustrate them.

DIFFERENTIATION

Strategy is concerned with developing competitive advantage, and competitive advantage achieves differentiation. Differentiation may be on the basis of any strategic factor or combination of them. It can take many forms. Each form is based on the selection of strategic factors upon which competitive advantage is built.

Competitive advantage and differentiation apply to all key stakeholders. For example, in the case of employees, an organization can differentiate itself on the basis of remuneration or on career prospects. In other words, it sets itself apart as regards strategic factors and becomes the employer of choice. In Chapter 9 we see how Bright Horizons, a child care company, has done just that.

There are no mysteries here. Differentiation means distinguishing ourselves from the competition, standing out from the crowd, being different in a way that appeals to our key stakeholders, be they customers or employees or suppliers or owners. And what is the basis of this difference? Strategic factors. So, understanding the strategic factors relevant to our key stakeholders gives us the basis for developing differentiation.

MONT BLANC

Mont Blanc, the maker of expensive pens, has differentiated itself on the strategic factors of price, product quality, range of goods sold, store presentation and image. Although a maker of classy fountain pens in Germany since 1908, the company only took off in a big way in the 1990s. This followed a move by the Vendome Luxury Group in 1987, which owns Mont Blanc, Cartier, Dunhill and Chloe — to name but a few of its well-recognized labels. At that time, the Group took a decision to defend Mont Blanc's position as a status brand.

Almost overnight, they discontinued 50% of the product lines, the cheaper 50%, and focused on their highly-priced Meisterstuck range. They also withdrew their pens from regular pen shops and distributed only to fancy retailers prepared to put the effort into elaborate displays. As they saw it, high price and limited distribution equaled exclusivity. They wanted to deal only with stores that could guarantee a good turnover and a strong display. The strategy worked. The company has seen a 400% growth in revenue since that time.

In keeping with Mont Blanc's image, it advertises in glossy magazines pitched at the right demographic. Like most luxury-goods retailers, they are not too interested in television advertising. Such advertising is seen as "too democratic" and not targeted enough.

Mont Blanc is an interesting example of differentiation along strategic factors. As noted already, its focus has been upon price, product quality, range of goods sold, store presentation and image. Its success has depended upon this focus as a competitive advantage. The consistency of performance across these strategic factors has delivered superior value in the view of its customers.

TAG HEUER

We now move from pens to watches, but the message is the same. Successful differentiation focuses on strategic factors.

TAG Heuer, the prestige watch company, has been campaigning aggressively for the last several years with glossy advertising campaign shots by photographers like Herb Ritts. The prestige watch trade is intensely competitive. TAG Heuer competes directly with brands like Rolex, Patek Philippe and Jaeger-Le-Coultre. All these watches are marketed with a high price and limited distribution.

Heuer was the company that split the second by one hundred in 1915. At that stage it was making a boxing stopwatch and a roulette stopwatch. However, it decided to concentrate less on stopwatches and more on wristwatches with a sporting image.

The company launched an international advertising campaign that used action shots from the sporting world. In 1987 it introduced a designer watch that allowed it to enter into Rolex territory. By the beginning of the 1990s, TAG Heuer had come from nowhere on the watch-selling charts to be number five in terms of market share by value. Its watches now sell for an average price of $1,700 and its top-of-the-range platinum watch sells for $70,000.

TAG Heuer is an organization that has differentiated itself through its brand. The strategic factors it has focused on are price, image and product quality. It has achieved competitive advantage based on these factors, and its customers have obtained superior value.

POSITIONING

The concept of positioning is one that is as familiar to the world of advertising, sales and marketing as it is to strategic planning. It can be an outcome of achieving competitive advantage and differentiation. A product or service becomes positioned in our minds on the basis of price, image, customer service or some other strategic factor. For example, Rolls Royce is positioned in our minds as a "prestige motor vehicle." A Rolex watch is positioned in our minds as an "expensive watch."

In all these instances, the organizations have made it part

of their strategy to emphasize certain strategic factors over others. Rolls Royce emphasizes, among other factors, price, image and product quality. This is the basis of its competitive advantage.

These examples show how strategic factors and their manipulation impact positioning, and how positioning is related to differentiation and competitive advantage. Let's now look at some more examples of positioning.

LEXUS

Lexus is a classic example of an organization thinking through the problems of positioning and deciding to build a new brand from scratch. Toyota wished to enter the prestige car market and decided that its own brand had been positioned in people's minds as "not prestige." It needed another brand, and Lexus was the name chosen.

Lexus, short for "Luxury Export to the US," was designed specifically for the US market. It's sold in its own upmarket dealerships, complete with expensive fittings, and by sales staff who are called executives. It has its own service centers, 24-hour help lines and special customer service programs, including at-your-door repair service.

Toyota spent $3 billion in the 1980s developing Lexus and researched everything from the market's preference for timber paneling to the look of the engine. It had teams of engineers and marketers living in luxury in California to research the West Coast lifestyle. Little cost was spared to convince motoring journalists that this was the luxury car of the future.

Positioning products and services means positioning them in our minds according to various attributes. Toyota had already been pigeonholed and the company correctly felt that extending its own brand to a luxury product would have been unsuccessful.

The strategic factors that Toyota had to come to grips with in this decision concerned price, image, product features and customer service. For success, all these factors had to be aligned. Toyota not only recognized this fact, but was able to achieve that alignment. It successfully positioned Lexus in our minds, differentiated itself from the competition, achieved superior value for its customers and won competitive advantage.

DAVID JONES

Positioning a department store in this era of specialization is a difficult task. There is no single blueprint. In such famous US stores as Bloomingdales, Macy's and Saks 5th Avenue, about 80% of stock is apparel and accessories, with home wares accounting for the remainder. In Australia, David Jones and Myer Grace run at about 50% apparel and accessories, with the rest in a wide range of home wares, electrical and other goods.

Positioning a department store is difficult because of the product range and, potentially at least, the wide variety of customers it caters for. David Jones, however, has flip-flopped in its positioning over recent years. Traditionally — and its history goes back 160 years — David Jones was seen as a high-quality, prestigious store set apart from its competitors. A few years ago, the company deliberately drifted down-market and began to compete on price. It took on its competitors at the bottom end of the market, such as Target and K-Mart. Standards of service also slipped, and employees as well as customers were confused.

The strategy has been to rediscover those strategic factors that located David Jones in its special position in people's minds. It now emphasizes product quality, customer service, its history, the quality brands it stocks, fashion parades and personalities. It is also considering location, different merchandising methods and point-of-sale techniques.

The upmarket move of Australia's traditional prestige department store has been achieved by focusing on strategic factors and positioning the organization accordingly. David Jones' share of the total Australian department store market has risen to just under 10%, after falling for five years.

Margins are also improving. The retailer hopes, through its strategy, to reposition its brand, differentiate itself from the competition, achieve superior value for its customers and obtain competitive advantage. So far it's working!

WOOL

Not all positioning is concerned with branded products and branded retail stores. Even government departments such as the Department of Social Security and the Department of Defense are positioned in our minds, based on strategic factors. The same is true for a commodity such as wool.

Wool is attempting to reposition itself in an increasingly competitive apparel market. The fiber is becoming uncompetitive on price and has an image as a formal fiber, to be used for suits, jackets, coats, warm clothes and carpets. The trend in clothing, however, is towards "casual," and casual clothing is increasingly made of cotton and synthetics.

Wool has become trapped by its own marketing endeavors to position the product as a prestigious one. It is increasingly being boxed into the high-price, low-growth end of the world fiber market. As a result, it is losing market share in its traditional markets and has not, at this stage, broken into new ones.

One way of repositioning wool is through innovative blends, such as wool plus Lycra, developed by Dupont; wool plus cotton; and wool plus Supriva. The material must be an effective protection against the cold and must make fine suits but, either alone or with blends, it must also lend itself to casual wear and easy care.

To sum up, the strategic factors wool is currently entrapped by are price, image and product utility. It hopes, through its repositioning strategy, to differentiate itself from competitive materials, achieve superior value for its buyers and win competitive advantage.

SEARS ROEBUCK

Another retailing example of repositioning is Sears Roebuck. Its strategy has moved the retail giant from a net loss of $3.9 billion in 1992 to a net profit in excess of $1.4 billion. The turnaround has been a result of refocusing the organization through a combination of strategic factors, including customer service, product range and price.

Sears Roebuck has a long history. It began as a small watch repair company in Chicago and developed into a nationwide catalog mail order business, famous for supplying hardware lines. By the 1930s Sears had grown into a broad-based merchandised catalog, carrying everything from clothing to tools, kit homes and jewelry.

But by the 1980s, the US retail environment had become more complex and certainly more competitive; organizations grew up that were known as "category killers." These were large, single-category stores and superstores that focused on a limited product range, but in depth. Wal-mart and K-mart were in this group.

By the early 1990s, Sears Roebuck had been written off as a retailing dinosaur.

Its repositioning involved winning over women aged 25 to 54. A number of moves were made, including the discontinuation of its catalog business — at least in the short term. Later the company re-launched the catalog business but, this time, with several targeted catalogs, rather than the one, all-inclusive version. It closed over one hundred poorly performing stores and cut 50,000 jobs. All non-core assets, such as insurance and financial services, were divested, and stores repositioned to change the perception of most female customers that Sears sold only hardware products. This move has seen its apparel business grow significantly.

Sears Roebuck achieved success by remaining focused on its target customer, the American woman aged 25 to 54. It learned that, as it had grown, it had become inwardly focused and had lost touch with its target customers. In our terms, it had approached strategy inside-out rather than outside-in. It had stagnated on traditional programs rather than continually renewing itself through the eyes of its customers.

By understanding the strategic factors pertinent to those customers, and securing competitive advantage relative to them, Sears Roebuck has become very successful once more. It has positioned itself successfully and achieved superior value.

ACCOR HOTELS

Accor Hotels' positioning is classic. The world's largest hotel network is home to 3,000 hotels in every category, from "budget to luxury," as they describe it. Accor operates five levels in pricing terms: Hotel Sofitel, Novotel, Mercure Hotel, Ibis Hotel and Motel Formule 1. Each of these hotels occupies a distinct position defined by price and performance on all other strategic factors. Here are some descriptions from Accor's directory that aptly illustrate positioning by strategic factors.

Hotel Sofitel is described as a hotel "where perfection is our obsession." The Sofitel is "committed to providing you with the impeccable standards and degree of comfort that is your right to expect." As the directory says, "we strive to give even your smallest request the closest attention, to take account of your particular requirements." Of course, we're not talking cheap here. The Hotel Sofitel operates at the high end of the hotel market.

The next level down in the Accor categories is the Novotel. The Novotel is the business person's hotel and, as the directory says, is "renowned as one of the world's leading business class brands." Novotels are not as expensive as Sofitel hotels nor do they provide the same range of services or as high a level of customer service. They are, as the directory puts it, "modern, stylish hotels located in prime business centers and popular resort destinations." They aim to attract the business person.

The Mercure Hotel is another step down in terms of price and other strategic factors. Again the directory reflects this.

It states that Mercure Hotels "reflect their local culture and enable you to discover the regional traditions of their respective countries." They provide "easily recognised levels of comfort and price."

Ibis Hotels are less expensive than Mercure Hotels and, as the directory says, "locations are always highly convenient. Rooms are pleasantly furnished in contemporary style, with functional bathrooms."

Motel Formule 1 is at the budget end of the hotel industry. "Motel Formule 1 set the standard in the economy class category," the directory informs us. Motel Formule 1 "guarantees the lowest-priced rooms wherever you go. Comfort is simple and functional, but guaranteed." While Motel Formule 1 is at the low price end of the market, it seeks to provide commensurate performance on all other strategic factors.

REPOSITIONING – IT ISN'T EASY

Sears Roebuck succeeded in repositioning itself in the minds of 25-to-54-year-old women, but repositioning definitely is not easy. The task for Sears was to reconnect with a disenchanted group of customers — disenchanted, but not disenfranchised, not completely disconnected from the organization. The company had probably not lost touch with this demographic, just temporarily turned it off.

Once strategic factors have become cemented in people's minds, changing their perceptions is a real challenge.

In attempting to reposition their organization and their brand, Sears Roebuck and others are dealing with the enduring and pervasive strategic factor of image and reputation, which occurs on lists for customers, employees, suppliers, owners. It's especially relevant with branded products and, even more, when those brands are high profile.

GALLO WINES

Gallo Wines is a case in point. It is wrestling with the strategic factor of image and reputation in launching its new brand, Gallo of Sonoma.

E. & J. Gallo Winery is now being run by the third generation of the Gallo family. A monster in the American wine market, it produces one in every four bottles of wine sold in the US and sells more than 60 million cases of wine each year. Nearly one in every three wine grapes grown in California is taken up by Gallo, and its sales in 1999 were $1.4 billion. Twice the size of the next biggest American winery, Canandaigua Brands, Gallo is known as the "Wal-Mart of the wine industry" because it has built its image around the low end of the market, the cheaper mass-produced wines.

Yet the US wine market has undergone a major shift in the past 10 years. Wines made from a particular variety, e.g. chardonnay, cabernet and zinfandel, topped sales for generic or blended wines for the first time in 1993. Now sales of premium varietal wines are growing at double-digit rates, while sales for bulk wine are shrinking.

Gallo knows that if it wants to continue to dominate the American wine market, it needs to adapt to these changing tastes. So it has tackled the strategic factor, *image and reputation*, and aspires to reposition itself in its consumers' minds.

What is it doing to appeal to the higher-priced end of the wine market? It launched a new brand, Gallo of Sonoma, in the Spring of 1999, spending an estimated $4 million on the campaign to inspire consumers to try it. The Gallo of Sonoma ranges from the basic varietal, such as a cabernet, zinfandel or chardonnay, priced at around $10 a bottle, to the mid-range $16 to $20 from a specific Gallo of Sonoma vineyard, to the top end, such as the Estate Chardonnay or Estate Cabernet, which are priced at $35 and up.

Gallo faces some serious obstacles, the central one being the difficulty of changing its performance on the "image and reputation" factor. It is asking its market to think not VW, but Mercedes Benz. This isn't easy! Once strategic factors have become cemented in people's minds, changing their perceptions is a real challenge.

DEVELOPING COMPETITIVE ADVANTAGE

In this chapter we've tackled fundamental concepts in value, competitive advantage, differentiation and positioning and have supplied a new approach to each. All are linked and have common roots: strategic factors.

At the heart of strategy lies competitive advantage. It is by developing that advantage on a set of strategic factors for a key stakeholder that the latter supports an organization or business unit over its competitors.

Competitive advantage is linked to the concept of value. Key stakeholders evaluate their transactions with an organization or business unit based on a set of strategic factors. Thus strategic factors drive value and value drives competitive advantage. In this way, organizations and business units differentiate themselves from the competition and take a position in key stakeholders' minds.

Perhaps until now value, competitive advantage, differentiation and positioning were unrelated in your mind. They seem to come from different sources, from strategic planning, from marketing, from advertising, from sales. This chapter has shown that they are *intimately* related to each other and, most importantly, are underpinned by strategic factors. We believe that the realization of this makes the concepts themselves more useful in strategy. They no longer seem like items on a shopping list.

The next chapter takes competitive advantage to its next stage, the design of strategy.

---

1   Connolly, P., "To Quit or Not to Quit," *Sunday Life!* 2001, April, 34.

CHAPTER 7

DOING WHAT YOU DO BETTER

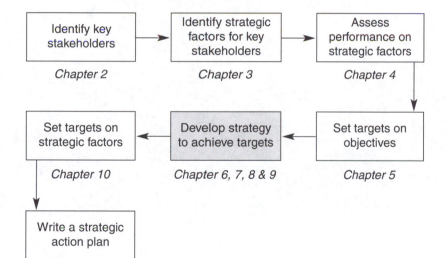

Identify key stakeholders	Identify strategic factors for key stakeholders	Assess performance on strategic factors
Chapter 2	*Chapter 3*	*Chapter 4*

Set targets on strategic factors	Develop strategy to achieve targets	Set targets on objectives
Chapter 10	*Chapter 6, 7, 8 & 9*	*Chapter 5*

Write a strategic action plan
Chapter 11

For many organizations one of the most difficult things in strategy development is to think of alternatives — strategic alternatives. They find themselves boxed in by competitors and sandwiched by the demands of certain stakeholders.

But an understanding of strategic factors has now widened your choices. There's a position *you* can occupy while your competitors can occupy theirs. The example of Accor Hotels with its numerous hotel brands and styles is a classic one.

The choices are defined by a combination of strategic factors.

There *is* a place for everyone, *provided* you get the right combination. High price and low product quality is a non-workable combination.

The aim of the current chapter is to take strategic choice further by classifying the complete range of strategic options, but concentrating particularly on one category, the one we call Scale Strategy.

This chapter and the next two tie together a number of apparently diverse and unrelated strategic activities. These include diversification, lobbying, acquisition, strategic alliance and innovation.

In these three chapters, you have the entire range of options and you can use them as a checklist in making your own choices and developing detailed strategies. In so doing, you'll see how these options are related to one another and to strategic factors.

If you will turn back to Figure 5.2, on page 73, the Strategy Development Funnel, you will see how strategy is wedged between key strategic issues and strategic factors. In developing strategy, we are influenced by those issues (already identified at this point), and we build strategy around strategic factors. In addition, the strategy we develop needs to achieve the targets we have set on objectives.

While Figure 5.2 shows a sequential progression from mission, vision and values to objectives and then to strategy, we have already noted that, in practice, it rarely flows this smoothly. For example, suppose a planning team had a

An understanding of strategic factors has widened your choices.

target to double sales in the next three years, but in attempting to develop strategy based on this objective, they realized how unrealistic it was. They would probably decide to go back and revise the target, reducing it to an achievable level.

THE THREE S'S OF STRATEGY

Listed below are the six strategic options faced by organizations and business units. Particular *strategies* are developed from within *each* option.

- improve performance in present industry;
- diversity/intensify across industries;
- lobby rule makers and change industry rules (lobbying);
- link up with supplier, buyer or competitor (strategic alliance);
- acquire supplier, buyer or competitor (acquisition);
- develop a breakthrough approach (innovation).

Figure 7.1 classifies these options according to the Three S's: Scale, Scope and Structure. Notice how the three strategy types are built around strategic factors and how each type has a fundamentally different way of describing its impact on strategic factors.

There are only three ways by which organizations and business units compete.

There are only three ways by which organizations and business units compete:

Scale Strategy occurs when you outperform the competition on existing strategic factors. Scale Strategy is concerned with finding depth, with concentrating effort on a few strategic factors, with focusing on those few factors that

Figure 7.1   **Summary of Strategic Options**

Strategy Type	Strategic Options
Scale • Outperform the competition on existing strategic factors	• Improve performance in present industry
Scope • Outperform the competition on changed strategic factors	• Diversify/intensify across industries
Structure • Change competitors' performance on strategic factors	• Lobby rule makers and change industry rules (lobbying) • Link up with supplier, buyer or competitor (strategic alliance) • Acquire supplier, buyer or competitor (acquisition) • Develop a breakthrough approach (innovation)

will make an organization or business unit successful.

Scope Strategy occurs when you choose different strategic factors and then outperform the competition. Scope Strategy is concerned with breadth. Here diversification becomes an issue.

> **Scale Strategy is concerned with finding depth, with concentrating effort on a few Strategic Factors.**

Structure Strategy occurs when you change your competitors' performance on strategic factors. In contrast to both Scale and Scope Strategy, Structure Strategy is concerned with outmaneuvering the competition by changing competitors' performance on strategic factors. It focuses on changing the structure of the relationship between an organization and its competitors.

The question generally being asked in Scale Strategy is: How deep do we wish to make our spe-

> **Scope Strategy is concerned with breadth.**

Structure Strategy aims to turn things upside down.

cialization? The question asked in Scope Strategy is: Over what range of industries should our organization or business unit compete? Structure Strategy aims to turn things upside down, to change the structure of relationships and the relevance of strategic factors.

The relationship between strategy types, strategic options and particular strategies is shown in Figure 7.2.

Figure 7.2   **Types, Options and Strategies**

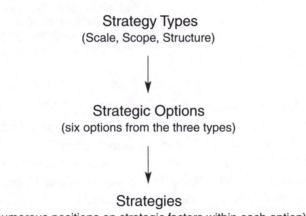

Strategy Types
(Scale, Scope, Structure)

Strategic Options
(six options from the three types)

Strategies
(numerous positions on strategic factors within each option)

In this chapter we examine the first of these Three S's of Strategy in detail and explain how you can apply this Scale Strategy effectively for your key stakeholders. But first let's make sure we understand what developing strategy by key stakeholder means.

STRATEGY BY KEY STAKEHOLDER

When you're developing strategy, whether it be Scale, Scope or Structure, do it by key stakeholder. This doesn't mean that they should be the ones to formulate the strategy, but rather that you should classify strategy according to key stakeholders — in other words, for customers, for suppliers, for employees and for owners.

This isn't the way strategy is usually developed, we must admit. Most organizations and business units tend to focus on customers, and take all other key stakeholders for granted. The risk is that when suppliers, for example, are taken for granted, they fall down on the job, and it is the customers who pay the ultimate price. When employees are taken for granted, things don't go right and, again, it is the customers who pay. When owners are taken for granted, the organization or business unit can starve for funds, and then everyone pays the price!

It's simply shortsighted to suggest that in developing strategy, certain key stakeholders should be ignored. Evidence shows, for instance, that organizations with a well-developed employee strategy significantly outperform those without it.

Take, for example, Solent, an importer of baby products. Where would it be without a clear and well-defined strategy for suppliers? Or take Peninsular Finance, a financial services provider. How would it fare if it only concentrated on customers? (Both of these organizations are real, but their names have been altered.)

SOLENT

Solent is a privately-owned company that imports baby products. These products include baby bottles, bottled accessories, teats, comforters, cups, teething aids, eating accessories and toys.

Solent set out to develop a strategic plan for its future. Once established, its planning team found that among its key strategic issues were the static market it faced and the powerful control of a few customers. The team also identified the need to develop strategy for all of its key stakeholders:

- Consumers
- Customers (retailers)
- Suppliers
- Employees
- Shareholders

It had to be clear about the strategic factors for each and eventually identified the following:

Consumers
- Price
- Product design (safety, innovation and performance)
- Brand
- Availability
- Packaging
- Consumer service

Customers
- Retail price (stock turnover)
- Margin
- Exclusive product
- Customer service
- National brands
- Information on supply chain costs

Suppliers
- Long production runs with minimum assortments
- Regular orders
- Long lead times
- New product ideas
- Consistent payment history
- Exclusive supplier of certain products
- Detailed product specifications
- Personal relationship

Employees
- Rewards
- Recognition
- Working conditions
- Corporate direction

Shareholders
- Company performance
- Brand performance
- Return on funds invested

With this understanding of its key stakeholders and the strategic factors relevant to each, the planning team set about developing strategy to achieve competitive advantage. But it did this for *each* of the company's key stakeholders and recognised linkages between them.

PENINSULAR FINANCE

Peninsular Finance is 50% owned by a large bank and offers financial planning advise to individuals of high net worth. In addition, it manages their funds.

Peninsular Finance wished to develop a strategic plan that took it forward into the ever-growing funds management industry. It identified the following key stakeholders and strategic factors:

Customers
- Brand reputation
- Quality of advice
- Quality of service
- Investment performance

Employees
- Inspiring and motivating leadership
- Meeting personal and professional needs and aspirations
- Ability to make a valuable contribution
- Opportunity to achieve maximum personal potential

Suppliers
- Terms and conditions
- Revision and maintenance of service standards
- Interchange of information
- Supplier/partner relationship

Shareholders
- Growth
- Value creation
- Company reputation
- Meeting joint venture initiatives
- Management's performance

This example also shows how different industries have different ways of expressing strategic factors. Peninsular Finance's own culture, as well as the culture of its industry, being largely highly skilled, the company expresses them differently from organizations in other industries. Also of note in the case of employees is how the strategic factors are clearly focused on its *current* employees.

Armed with this information, the strategic planning team set about developing strategy and achieving competitive advantage with each of its key stakeholders.

SCALE STRATEGY

In one sense, we have already covered Scale Strategy, since we discussed how organizations outperform the competition by building competitive advantage on one or more strategic factors in their industry (Chapter 6).

You might also recall that we supplied a number of examples of differentiation and positioning based on strategic factors, to achieve competitive advantage. They were examples of Scale Strategy in action.

Mont Blanc differentiated itself on price, product quality, range of goods, store presentation and image. Because it stayed within its own field, the writing pen industry, its strategy was a Scale Strategy.

TAG Heuer, too, stayed within its own watch industry. It differentiated itself from its competition and achieved competitive advantage on price, image and product quality. Again this is Scale Strategy, since TAG Heuer aims to outperform the competition on existing strategic factors and not diversify into other industries.

One of the examples provided for positioning was Lexus. The Lexus car is also an example of Scale Strategy, since Toyota sought to gain competitive advantage in the car industry with the Lexus brand. Here again, the advantage was built on price, image, product features and customer service. Competitive advantage was sought by outperforming the competition on existing strategic factors.

We have talked about how department store David Jones sought competitive advantage by positioning itself on product quality, customer service and image. This, too, was an example of Scale Strategy, since the company wished to stay within the department store industry. Likewise, Sears Roebuck followed Scale Strategy by seeking competitive advantage in the minds of American women aged 25 to 54, without moving outside its industry.

To illustrate Scale Strategy further, let's consider another, well-known example:

McDONALD'S

McDonald's is an organization that has always been focused on strategic factors and has developed through Scale Strategy. It has built its competitive advantage around a few areas important to its customers.

As a market leader in its field, it prides itself on striving to achieve:

- quality
- service
- cleanliness
- value.

From the beginning, all McDonald's stores have been regularly measured on their performance in the above four areas. How they rate affects store managers' compensation and, in fact, poor performance on these can lead to a manager being fired or to loss of a franchise.

In strategic factor terms, what are quality, service, cleanliness and value? Are they the only ingredients of McDonald's success?

Quality, service, cleanliness and value are strategic factors for customers, one of the key stakeholders. However, this is not the full list of strategic factors for them. The full list of seven is shown in Figure 7.3 below, with the four factors above having been altered to comply with the terminology employed in this book. Also shown is a performance rating for McDonald's on each of the seven.

Figure 7.3 **Performance Rating of McDonald's on Strategic Factors**

Strategic Factor	Performance Rating
• Product quality ("quality")	• Characterized by consistency between stores and globally — exceeds the competition.
• Customer service ("service")	• Set benchmarks on friendly and efficient service in fast food restaurants — exceeds the competition.
• Store presentation ("cleanliness")	• McDonald's emphasizes cleanliness as the key feature of its store presentation — clearly competitive in this regard.
• Price ("value")	• McDonald's prefers the term "value" to de-emphasize price. Price is competitive, though not necessarily the cheapest.

- Range of products
  - McDonald's has experimented with a variety of goods over the years, but its range at the present time seems to meet the needs and expectations of its customers. Not listed by management with the four factors of quality, service, value and cleanliness, since it is not something that employees control.

- Location
  - McDonald's does not emphasize this as part of its credo, since location is not controlled by its employees. However, location is vital and their location decisions have certainly made McDonald's competitive.

- Image/brand values
  - One of the strongest barriers to entry for any competitor is McDonald's reputation and brand, especially with its youthful customers. It has spent millions of dollars creating its image, and its reputation is one of the important ingredients of McDonald's success. It has enabled it to obtain a major "share of mind" and to position itself as synonymous with fast food.

The performance ratings above are a summary evaluation of McDonald's on the strategic factors relevant to fast-food customers. In a major way, its success has been due to the ability to identify correctly the strategic factors pertaining to its industry. It can also be attributed to placing the right emphasis on those factors as far as customers are concerned.

Product quality — that is, consistency of the product over time and throughout its stores — has been a major factor in attracting customers. McDonald's customer service has set industry standards, as has the presentation of its stores. Pricing for McDonald's has been consistent with the rest of its package. Its range of products — burgers, fries, etc. — has been such as to meet the needs of its customers. (Actually, McDonald's has had difficulty trying to move its customers to a broader range of products by the introduction of different tastes and flavors. Its customer base seems hooked on the current range of products.)

McDonald's spends considerable time on its selection of

locations, another strategic factor. (The story goes, falsely we might add, that McDonald's is in the "real estate business" because of the astuteness of its site selection over the years.)

Finally, but by no means least, McDonald's performance on image/brand values provides an enormous buffer against the competition.

McDonald's follows Scale Strategy continually, focusing on achieving competitive advantage on existing strategic factors, i.e., those relevant to its industry.

Of course, the company's current success is not a guarantee for the future. Indeed, the seeds of failure are sometimes sown in success. McDonald's, one of the world's best-known brands, is synonymous with burgers and fries. What if burgers and fries become unfashionable? What if people's tastes and preferences move to other foods? Can McDonald's, the brand, move as well?

These are questions that take us into the territory of Scope Strategy, and we deal with this in the next chapter. For now, we consider Devon Dairy (not its real name) and demonstrate Scale Strategy *applied along its industry value chain.*

DEVON DAIRY

The list below was derived from a much larger list of stakeholders for Devon Dairy, many of whom, on balance, were not considered "key." This example has been chosen because it differs from the conventional business organization in interesting and important ways.

Devon Dairy is a dairy cooperative and has a turnover of a billion dollars. Its products include milk, which it packages and sells to retailers via vendors and distributors, and manufactured milk products such as ice cream, yogurt and savory dips.

The key stakeholders of Devon Dairy are:

- Farmers
  - shareholders

- – suppliers
- Vendors/distributors
- Customers
  - – retail
  - – industrial/food service
- Consumers
- Employees

It is an unusual but intriguing organization; being a cooperative, the suppliers of the milk (i.e. the farmers) are also the shareholders of the organization. Thus the farmers occupy the two roles of *supplier* and *shareholder*. What is also of note is how the expectations of farmers have to be considered separately in these two roles and how strategy has to be developed separately *for each role*.

The milk and milk products are distributed to Devon Dairy's customers by independently owned *vendors/distributors*. These vendors/distributors are small businesses in their own right.

One set of *customers* involves organizations at retail level (supermarkets and convenience stores) who buy the milk and other products to sell to consumers. Another set of customers comprises industrial organizations that wish to reprocess the product further and so buy in bulk, and food service organizations such as restaurants. The expectations of each set of customers are quite different. While supermarkets and convenience stores expect their milk in suitably sized and labeled containers, some restaurants want their milk packaged in plastic bags that fit their particular food distribution machines.

Consumers are also a key stakeholder. They are the individuals and families who consume the product and who, in the end, decide whether it is worthwhile. The product, such as milk, goes from the dairy cooperative into the hands of the vendors/distributors, on to the customers (supermarkets and convenience stores), and only then to the consumer. Strategy must be developed at each of the three points in the distribution chain: vendors/distributors, customers, and consumers. To concentrate on only one point and ignore the others will lead to ineffective strategy.

Finally we come to *employees*. No other stakeholders will receive satisfaction without effective performance from employees. Strategy must be developed to ensure that Devon Dairy attracts capable employees and that these employees maintain their effort.

Even though it may not control performance on all the strategic factors in the vendor/customer interaction or the customer/consumer interface, it nonetheless needs to develop strategy to ensure that its products flow successfully from itself to its consumers. In other words, it needs to achieve superior performance to competitors on one or more of the factors that apply. This is, of course, Scale Strategy.

Strategy for Vendors/Distributors

The strategic factors for vendor/distributors in their relationship with Devon Dairy are:

- Vendor service
- Product quality
- Vendor security and profitability
- Product range
- Fee.

Vendor service involves Devon Dairy's handling of orders, administration and communication. Vendors expect it to perform well on this factor, just as on product quality. They rely on it to maintain high standards for its product, because this affects their relationships with their customers. As their relationship with Devon Dairy is a contractual one, vendors are also concerned about their security and profitability. And the range of products available to them is another strategic factor: it affects their viability and income. Finally, fee refers to the money paid to vendors/distributors for cartage, and this, too, is naturally a strategic factor for them.

The strategy Devon Dairy developed around vendor service concerned improving order consistency, reducing the amount of administration required from vendors and improving communication via modern technology. Strategy related to product quality focused on maintaining Devon Dairy's superior position on quality. This was accomplished by investing in equipment and training programs, which improved freshness and package integrity. The strategy around vendor security and profitability involved developing partnership agreements with guarantees for the vendors/distributors.

On product range, Devon Dairy recognized the need to secure products complementary to existing ones in order to improve vendor viability and profitability. Hence it broadened its product range.

In each instance, we can see Devon Dairy seeking to achieve competitive advantage via strategic factors in its present industry and bind its vendors/distributors to it. It wants to avoid having those distributors desert to the competition or quit the industry altogether. So it aims to provide value superior to anything the vendors/distributors could get elsewhere.

Strategy for Customers

The strategic factors for customers (retail stores) in their relationship with vendors/distributors are:

- Trading terms
- Product range
- Delivery
- Customer service.

The retail stores provide an interesting example of key stakeholders in a value chain where strategic factors are influenced jointly by two organizations further up the chain, namely, Devon Dairy and the vendors/distributors. Trading terms and product range are almost totally controlled by Devon Dairy. Delivery is almost totally controlled by the vendors/distributors. And customer service is jointly controlled by Devon Dairy and the vendors/distributors.

Scale Strategy was set accordingly. In the case of trading terms, Devon Dairy developed focused trading terms that reflected each customer's unique relationship and incorporated joint growth and profit targets. On customer service and delivery, it improved distribution efficiency and engaged in joint promotional activity with retail customers. It also broadened its product range by adding additional products, such as more flavors of yogurt.

Strategy for Consumers

The strategic factors for consumers in their relationship with customers are:

- Image
- Availability
- Price
- Packaging
- Product range.

Devon Dairy's strategy was constructed around raising the image of its brand and building brand awareness. It developed relevant and clear product benefits for its major brand and rationalized surplus brands without losing revenue. As for availability, Devon Dairy ensured that consumers could readily obtain its product from retail stores. Its strategy on price was to see to it that its pricing was in line with consumer tolerance and consistent with brand positioning, while maximizing its own revenue.

Packaging was given desirable attributes that met consumer needs: distinctive, easy to find and easy to use, providing information for consumers. It also met environmental standards that paralleled consumer expectations.

In the case of product range, Devon Dairy sought to preempt consumer needs by monitoring local and international food and beverage trends. It aimed to keep its top spot in the market with innovative, yet profitable, products and set about launching one completely new product each year.

Through all these strategies, Devon Dairy made every effort to deliver value to consumers that was superior to that of other dairy product producers or producers of products that compete with dairy products, such as fruit drinks and confectioneries.

This example illustrates Scale Strategy at each point in a value chain. To make it effective, strategic factors need to be understood and addressed and competitive advantage achieved at these points in order to ensure that products or services continue to move down the value chain and the organization prospers and grows. (For a more detailed description of a value chain and further examples, see Appendix C, "Competitive Advantage Along Value Chains.")

> **Scale Strategy must be developed for the key stakeholders in a value chain.**

SCALE STRATEGY – A LOGICAL STARTING POINT

This chapter has introduced Strategy's Three S's and has concentrated on one, Scale Strategy. Its focus is to improve performance on the strategic factors that exist in an organization's present industry. We have shown how Scale Strategy can be extended to the key stakeholders in the industry value chain of an organization or business unit.

Scale Strategy is the logical place to start; thinking about how your organization can obtain competitive advantage by *doing better what it currently does* makes much sense. For one thing, it's highly likely that this will be your most cost-effective strategy. It doesn't involve diversification, which is the subject of Scope Strategy, nor does it involve acquisition and strategic alliances which, among other options, are elements in Structure Strategy.

However, although you start with developing Scale Strategy, you mustn't stop there! You need to press on to the other two.

CHAPTER 8

WHY DIVERSIFICATION IS NOT A STRATEGY

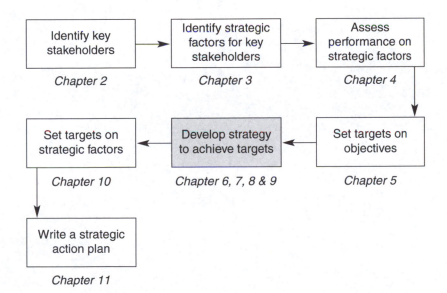

Scope Strategy is about diversification and is the focus of this chapter.

Diversification has its detractors, their opinions being fuelled by the history of failure associated with it, especially where diversification has been sought through acquisition. As this chapter will show in the case of Burns Philp, diversification involving large, and therefore risky, acquisitions can indeed have disastrous consequences.

It's important to note that we're concerned here with industry diversification, not the broadening of a product range — which some people refer to as diversification. An organization engages in industry diversification if it extends its efforts over more than one industry. For example, Semco is a manufacturer of industrial products *and* a provider of office maintenance services.

Diversification as applied to a product or service range, on the other hand, focuses on a strategic factor for customers; broadening it would come under Scale Strategy.

Our experience tells us that most organizations have difficulty with diversification. They don't know which way to turn. They're either so scared of the topic that they don't give it a second thought, or they're so unaware of the dangers they simply rush in.

Since neither extreme is really suitable, what is an appropriate approach to the issue? The answer lies in the

Our experience tells us that most organizations have difficulty with diversification.

description of Scope Strategy itself: it involves knowing strategic factors in the new industry.

SCOPE STRATEGY

Unlike Scale Strategy, where competitive advantage is built on strategic factors in an organization's or business unit's present industry, Scope Strategy is concerned with developing competitive advantage on *different* strategic factors. In other words, Scope Strategy involves taking a decision to move the company's activity to a different industry and then developing competitive advantage therein.

When we say a different industry, we are not necessarily thinking of a move from manufacturing to hotel services! The change of industry can be more subtle than that, as will be seen shortly in the case of a chain of gift stores, Gracious Gifts.

In Scale Strategy we're looking for depth of competitive advantage on strategic factors; in Scope Strategy, we're looking for breadth. We broaden the organization's industry focus.

Scope Strategy and Diversification

The strategic option listed in Figure 7.1 for Scope Strategy is "diversify/intensify across industries." We know that *diversification* involves broadening the activities of an organization; *intensification*, by contrast, means narrowing activities. Intensification is quite common these days; organizations are returning to "core business" and casting aside "non-core activities."

Diversification and intensification are two sides of the same coin. We will concentrate on diversification, because its successful implementation has been such a problem.

What if an organization or business unit has assessed that its industry does not have a great future? For example, a number of new competitors may be about to enter the market, or perhaps growth has slowed. It may be that a new technology has sprung up that will make certain products or services obsolete. Under these conditions, an organization or business unit may choose to diversify.

It's important to realize that in our terms, diversification is not a strategy. Strategy involves achieving competitive advantage precisely on the strategic factors themselves. Diversification, by itself, does not do this, so it cannot be a strategy.

History shows the unfortunate consequences of thinking of diversification as a strategy. Many organizations have followed this route with the thought that the "grass is greener on the other side of the fence" — only to find that it is in fact "scorched earth." Other industries often look more attractive than one's own from afar, but prove not so attractive at all once they are entered.

If diversification is not a strategy, then what is it? We would say that it *is a means of finding new strategy*. Note the wording of the "Scope" definition in Figure 7.1: "Outperform the competition on changed strategic factors." The emphasis here is on strategic factors. If we are to diversify, we must be well aware of what we are doing. When we choose different strategic factors, we *actually create a problem*. That problem is: How do we obtain competitive advantage on the strategic factors relevant to this new industry?

> **Diversification is not a strategy but a means of finding new strategy.**

In effect, by diversifying we're back to square one. We're back to the problem we had with Scale Strategy. If we're not careful, however, we compound it. We now have not one problem, but two: one in our existing industry, where we have to develop Scale Strategy, and one in the new industry, where we have to develop additional strategy, on a new set of strategic factors.

It is easy to see why diversification must be thought of not as strategy, but as a stepping-stone to the development of strategy.

The next three examples offer a cautionary tale, in the case of Gracious Gifts (not its real name); a disaster, in Burns Philp; and a success story, in Semco.

GRACIOUS GIFTS

To illustrate Scope Strategy, let's consider the chain of gift stores called Gracious Gifts. It sells craft products, such as pottery and other handmade items, by the normal retail methods. Now it has decided to diversify into the mail order industry because the constraints of the retail gift shop industry are such that, even if the store improves its performance on the six relevant strategic factors, it foresees little chance of good returns.

This assessment has been made on the basis of the industry's structure. Management believes margins will always be forced down by the arrival of more and more price-cutting competitors.

However, diversification brings its own problems, one of which is that management must identify and understand fully the strategic factors that pertain to the mail order industry. In addition, some of the factors pertinent to retail will no longer apply in the case of mail order. Look at the list below.

- Location (not relevant in mail order)
- Hours of operation (not relevant in mail order)
- Customer service (differently defined in mail order)
- Range of goods sold (still relevant, but only for mail order products)
- Store presentation (not relevant in mail order)
- Price (still relevant, but only for mail order products)

This list shows how many of the strategic factors, on which Gracious Gifts may have already developed strengths, become neutralized through diversification. Furthermore, diversification brings a number of other factors that will have to be developed. One of these is delivery.

Diversification can only be successful if it delivers competitive advantage on strategic factors.

Thus, in spite of diversifying, management still has to face the problem of how to outperform the competition. That problem has not gone away.

Diversification can only be successful if it delivers competitive advantage on strategic factors. When viewed this way, the task of successfully diversifying can certainly be seen as difficult. In the following example, diversification led to disastrous consequences.

BURNS PHILP

Burns Philp is an Australian-based multinational. In 1983, it contained 175 businesses, which ranged from wholesale merchants to finance, to film processors and everything in between.

In 1984, its Chief Executive had more than 50 managers reporting to him and, between that year and 1996, sold businesses and investments worth $1.3 billion and bought businesses worth $1.7 billion.

It was in the refocusing of Burns Philp that the seeds of its demise were sown. It had expertise in yeast production, being a world leader in this field. Deciding to diversify into antibiotics, it invested $195 million in 1987 in the purchase of an Italian antibiotics business. It spent another $100 million when environmental problems required building a new factory. From this initial investment of $295 million, however, success did not flow. So in 1995, the Italian business was sold for $44 million — a loss of close to $250 million.

The other area Burns Philp saw as a diversification opportunity was spices. It decided to break into the US market. But to do this, it needed to take on McCormick & Co., which held a 30% share of the spices market. Burns Philp was also in spices, in Germany, and the competitors in both countries fought back.

In the United States the battle took the form of escalating payments to retailers in order to get the best positions on supermarket shelves. These "slotting fees" cost Burns Philp $25 million in 1993 and $65 million in 1997. McCormick appeared to be prepared to "fight to the death."

The result was that both the antibiotics and the spices business were disasters for Burns Philp. It had a good business in 1983 and it still has that business, a proprietary technology for the production of yeast. It took its world market share in yeast from 1% in 1981 to 7% in 1990 and to more than 16% today. Indeed, it is a global leader in this business. But it mistook the connection between yeast and spices and antibiotics. The strategic factors that pertain to being a world leader in yeast do not necessarily translate into being an effective distributor of spices to retail stores and supermarkets, or an effective competitor in the antibiotics market. The one is quite different from the other.

The upshot of all this is that Burns Philp is now a shadow of its former self. Its market capitalization has dropped disastrously. It has not paid a dividend for several years and has struggled to survive.

SEMCO

Diversification doesn't have to be a disaster, as Semco illustrates. But the difference in Semco's and Burns Philip's experience is marked.

Firstly, Semco diversifies organically, not by acquisition. Secondly this organic diversification is achieved with partners that are already experienced in the new industry.

Let's take a look at Semco's story.

Semco is a Brazilian-based manufacturer, service provider and now digital company. Over the last ten years, it has grown steadily, quadrupling its revenue and increasing the number of employees from 450 to 1,300.

When it commenced in the early '90s, Semco manufactured products such as pumps, industrial mixers and dishwashers. In the last decade, it has successfully diversified into high-margin services, and almost 75% of its business now comes from the provision of services. It's diversifying further into e-business and expects that in the near future a quarter of its revenues will come from Internet activities.

Semco's transformation is an interesting one. Ten years ago one of the things it manufactured was cooling towers for large commercial buildings. But it expanded that business into managing cooling tower maintenance. It moved from manufacturing to services.

This addition of a major service component to its core business of manufacturing was further expanded when it provided maintenance services for air-conditioning compressors, and further still, when it took over all maintenance services for its customers. This included the addition of cleaning, security and general maintenance.

To do this, Semco sought a partner. It found Rockefeller Group's Cushman & Wakefield division, one of the largest real estate and property management companies in the United States. It formed a 50/50 joint venture with this organization in Brazil. Today, five years after its commencement, the joint venture has a revenue of $30 million.

There are many reasons for the success of this diversification, but a major one is that Semco took on a partner with an understanding of the business it wished to diversify into. Cushman & Wakefield understood the property management industry; Semco understood local Brazilian conditions.

This combined knowledge led to a clear grasp of strategic factors, and competitive advantage was built around them. Three are of particular note: price, range of services and customer service. On price, Semco was innovative. Instead of charging a flat fee based on a building's area, they developed a partnership model through which the charge was based on the savings made by its corporate customers.

It also provided a range of services that gave it a competitive advantage. For example, for one customer, it took over the tasks of 126 sub-contractors providing a wide range of maintenance and security services — from changing light bulbs to managing a fleet of cars to maintaining elevators. Semco provided all these services under one roof. It backed its good performance on price and range of services with excellent customer service.

Semco has now further diversified into eight Internet ventures. Interestingly though, they have grown directly out of the earlier service initiatives. Again, in diversifying, Semco has made sure to take partners along with it. Let's look at a couple of examples. In the case of facility management, it linked up with Johnson Controls. In inventory management, it linked up with the largest inventory-tracking company in the world, RGIS. It now has a web-enabled inventory control system that assists companies online to coordinate the fulfilment of electronic orders. The list goes on to the point where Semco is revolutionizing the construction process in Brazil. It has established a 50/50 joint venture with the US Internet software company, Bidcom, and has created a South American Web portal for the entire building industry. Semco makes its money by charging transaction fees on all business that takes place through the portal.

This company is an example of successful diversification but its interpretation of its success differs from ours. Its founder, Ricardo Semler, claims that Semco "went digital without a strategy." He places the emphasis for his organization's success on faith in people and letting employees take initiatives.

Important as these elements are in Semco's case, it's how Semco's employees have applied this autonomy that is of interest here. Firstly, we see that growth has occurred organically, not by acquisition. This allows Semco's employees to *learn*, and what do they learn? They learn about the industries into which they are diversifying. They learn gradually and they can correct their mistakes as they occur; usually, the mistakes aren't cataclysmic. Their insurance policy is that they learn the strategic factors relevant to the industries into which they diversify.

The other key to Semco's success with diversification is that it encourages partnering. They "partner promiscuously," to quote Semco. Whenever the company starts a new business, it always does so by seeking a partner. One advantage of this is that Semco is able to draw on the depth of partners' experience, which relates to an understanding of strategic factors relevant to the new business.

To sum up then, Semco's success has been diversification based on patience. It's patient in the way it approaches growth, i.e. organically, and it's patient in the way it approaches its diversification opportunities in that it takes time with its partners to understand the relevant strategic factors.

One further note about Semco and its diversification philosophy. Semler claims "that he has no idea of what business Semco is in and he doesn't want to know." This is an unusual management philosophy. For all of Semco's obvious strengths, including its CEO, there are dangers here.

At what point does it become an investment banker investing in its own businesses, diverse though they are, and lose the intimate knowledge of strategic factors required of an industry specialist? Contrast this to a company such as Nestlé, the world's largest food company, that steadfastly stays within the food industry. As Semco is a work in progress, we watch its future eagerly.[1]

SCOPE AND DIVERSIFICATION

Diversification is a formidable task — made all the more formidable because of its litany of failures. Yet it doesn't have to be this way; it can be approached sensibly. Scope Strategy is the sensible way, as it is entirely focused on strategic factors, with diversification merely the stepping-stone.

> **Scope Strategy is entirely focused on strategic factors, with diversification merely the stepping stone.**

This reversal in thinking about diversification is significant; it becomes a means of finding strategy. Strategy in our System is still built on strategic factors, and achieving competitive advantage on these is just as difficult in a new industry as it is in the current one. If diversification is on the agenda, continually asking questions about strategic factors should avoid disaster.

Strategy development shouldn't stop at Scale and Scope, however. Otherwise, additional strategic opportunities could be missed. How to avoid naive strategy is the subject of the next chapter.

---

1   Semler, R., "How We Went Digital Without a Strategy," *Harvard Business Review*, 2000, September-October, 51-58.

CHAPTER 9

AVOIDING
NAIVE STRATEGY

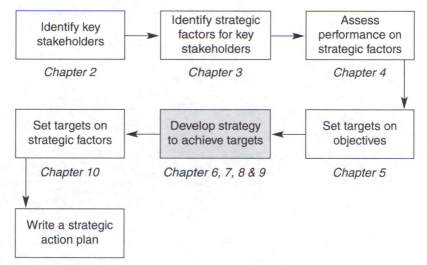

We've all heard the saying: work smarter, not harder. This applies to strategy.

For most organizations the emphasis in strategy development is upon improving performance *in what they currently do*. Of course this is admirable and may be highly successful — especially if the guidelines in Chapter 7, devoted to Scale Strategy, are followed.

But these organizations and their managers miss golden opportunities to pursue success. They down tools when they should plow on. They are being naive: they're working harder, but they're *not* working smarter.

It serves organizations well to be a little tricky here. For example, to lobby for what they want or form strategic alliances may be highly effective strategic maneuvers. Yet many shy away from such options because they don't normally think of them, or they don't see them as their legitimate domain.

In this chapter we dispel such notions and urge managers *not* to be naive, but rather to consider and pursue, where effective, Structure Strategy.

Structure Strategy is concerned with *outmaneuvering* not outperforming the competition, and it relates to both existing and different

Don't be naive, pursue all strategic options.

strategic factors. In other words, Structure Strategy may be applied to an organization's existing industry or to an industry into which it may be considering a move.

Structure Strategy is concerned with turning relationships upside down — rotating those that may already have been established by competitors. The four strategic options relevant to Structure Strategy, already shown in Figure 7.1, are reproduced below. Each of them will be discussed in this chapter.

- lobbying
- strategic alliance
- acquisition
- innovation

Structure Strategy involves holding performance on present strategic factors, but still outperforming the competition by use of any of the ways itemised above.

Structure Strategy involves changing your competitors' performance!

LOBBYING

We see the first of these options, *lobbying*, going on around us all the time. But it is rarely addressed in books on strategy. Look at what Japanese organizations have achieved in opposing potential exports to Japan. The non-tariff barriers erected by the Japanese government and lobbied for by Japanese organizations have kept potential exporters out of Japan and successfully neutralized the performance of many competitors, e.g. American exporters to Japan. Or take the way in which American primary producers have lobbied and received support and protection from the United States government against potential exporters of primary products from nations such as Australia.

In these instances, rules are changed so that the nature of the game favors one player over another. In the case of Japanese producers of electrical equipment, the non-tariff barriers ensure that no change in performance is required along strategic factors; the producers' competitive advantage is ensured by the rules.

At the same time, the non-tariff barriers have neutralized the performance of foreign competitors along those same strategic factors. The barriers stifle the ability of competitors to deliver their products to the Japanese market.

The use of tariffs in the case of European primary producers is another example of rules favoring local producers over overseas competitors. Those rules are held in place through lobbying.

These examples of lobbying relate to large organizations operating on a global scale, whose agents are national governments. However, Structure Strategy applies equally to small firms, e.g., convenience stores. You ask, what could a local store manager do in terms of lobbying that would neutralize the effectiveness of the competition?

Take the strategic factor, "location," as an example. The manager could lobby the relevant local government organization to place "no standing" signs outside nearby stores, with the excuse that they are on busy roads. Were this to occur, any location advantage held by a competitor of our convenience store would be neutralized. The manager would thus have achieved an advantage without having to improve his performance on the location factor or any other.

> **Through lobbying we change competitors' performance on strategic factors.**

The beauty of the convenience store example is that it highlights how lobbying is not confined to large organizations. Rules can be changed at a local level by small businesses — the impact on competition is the same. Through lobbying, we engage in Structure Strategy: changing competitors' performance on strategic factors. The wonderful thing about this type of Structure Strategy, as we saw in the example, is that it doesn't require us to change our performance on those same strategic factors.

STRATEGIC ALLIANCE

Another way in which competitors' performance on strategic factors can be changed is via a *strategic alliance*, which involves two organizations or business units cooperating for mutual benefit. We saw this already in the case of Semco and its joint venture arrangements. Another example could occur in the case of a trustee organization, which looks after the wills of its deceased clients. It might establish alliances with lawyers, so that certain of the trustee's work is assigned to them (e.g., property conveyancing) and, in return, the lawyers assign certain estate management work to the trustee. The formation of strategic alliances like this hampers the competition, to the mutual benefit of both allies.

Strategic alliances usually involve the combining of complementary strengths. Pepsico, for instance, with its strengths in the marketing of canned beverages, joined with Lipton, a recognized tea brand, to sell an iced tea jointly. Kentucky Fried Chicken, an already established brand with an established store format and operations skills, combined with Mitsubishi, whose strengths lay in real estate and site selection in Japan, to establish a KFC chain in that country.

Siemens, whose strengths lay in a range of telecommunications markets worldwide and in cable manufacturing technology, joined with Corning, whose strengths lay in optical fibers and glass, to create a fiber-optic-cable business. Ericsson, whose strengths lay in public telecommunication networks, joined with Hewlett-Packard, whose strengths were in computers, software and electronics, to create and market network management systems.

Strategic alliances are just that – alliances – and they don't last forever. They're set up to change competitors' performance on strategic factors by providing competitive advantage to the allies. Once this competitive advantage is delivered, the alliance may be disbanded. Its job has been done: both parties are now well established in their marketplace, and competitors have been warded off.

The formation of strategic alliances hampers the competition, to the mutual benefit of both allies.

The fact that they are not permanent arrangements is a plus for strategic alliances. If things don't work out, the parties can walk away from the alliance. Or, if it achieves its aims, the alliance can be wound up. This is not so with the next option in Structure Strategy, acquisition.

ACQUISITION

A further way by which organizations or business units

change competitors' performance on strategic factors is through *acquisition*. An organization may acquire its supplier or one of the immediate buyers in its distribution chain or one of its competitors. In each case, acquisition leads to a change in competitors' performance.

Acquisition may also operate to change industry structure. Rivalry among existing firms and the bargaining power of buyers and suppliers may be altered fundamentally by an acquisition. There is now less need for the acquiring company to change, especially to change performance on strategic factors.

Competition from a business can be eliminated by simply acquiring the business. The need to improve performance is then dramatically lessened. And if the acquired company were the only competitor in the industry, the acquirer now becomes a monopoly for the industry's customers. At this point, the need to improve performance on strategic factors for customers almost disappears. But this is an extreme case.

Let's suppose that a business acquires one competitor out of several. The acquiring organization has now taken some of the pressure off itself to improve its performance. And it has changed all the competitors' performance on strategic factors, too, because by incorporating one of its competitors into itself, it has lessened the market power of those remaining.

This same shift in power can be observed when an organization acquires the immediate buyer of its products. Take, for example, the cigarette company that purchased a major distributor, whose role was to deliver the cigarette company's and competitors' products to retail stores and supermarkets. By this purchase, the cigarette company was able to ensure that its products were given preference in the distribution channel. This changed the competitiveness of other cigarette companies that had been using this distributor to get their products onto retail shelves. Most importantly for the acquirer, it did not have to lift its performance on the strategic factors. It did not have to improve its customer service, its product quality, its branding and so on.

Acquiring a supplier is another way in which an organization can change competitors' performance on strategic factors. One instance is the concrete company that acquired its supplier of aggregates for concrete (a quarry company). It was then able to ensure that this supplier did not provide aggregates to the concrete company's competitors. By this action, it changed the cost structure of one of its competitors and hence, that competitor's ability to hold its prices down. The impact is obvious. At the same time, the acquirer itself has continued to carry on in much the same way as before. It didn't change the quality of its product, or its delivery or its customer service.

Acquisition changes the performance of competitors on strategic factors by changing industry structure.

We now look at two detailed examples of acquisition, aimed at changing the performance of competitors on strategic factors and hence the acquirer's competitive position.

DAIMLER CHRYSLER

Some observers believe that the automotive industry is set to consolidate from forty car companies to twenty in the twenty-first century. This consolidation, they say, is driven by the emergence of the global economy and the need for car manufacturers to be intercontinentally based.

The merger of Daimler Benz and Chrysler was the largest merger in automotive history and it reshaped an industry, with car makers scrambling to find partners to ensure their survival. It is a powerful example of two organizations consolidating to change an industry's strategic factors.

The merger brought together two giants. Daimler Benz is Germany's biggest industrial concern, and Chrysler is America's number three car maker. Daimler Chrysler also unites two of the world's most *profitable* car companies, with combined net earnings at the time of the merger of around $4.6 billion. In many ways the merger is a curious one: Mercedes Benz passenger cars are synonymous with engineering excellence and luxury, whereas Chrysler is well known for its low-cost production of trucks, minivans and utility vehicles. Chrysler is domestically based, whereas Mercedes is already global.

One aim of the merger, apart from consolidation and market power, was filling each company's product and geographic gaps. And, as neither company has a significant presence in Latin America or Asia, one of its first ventures is likely to be a small car to sell into the Asian and Latin American markets.

While we know that mergers often don't produce the synergies expected, Daimler Chrysler is a case where the combined entity hopes to reshape an industry through its market power and reduce competitors' performance on strategic factors. Only time will tell whether the diverse nature of the two companies will prevent the anticipated competitive advantage.

In the next example, we move from cars to chemicals — the pharmaceutical industry, to be specific, and the part that consolidations have played in it.

ROCHE

Pharmaceutical consolidations have become common in recent times. As in the motor vehicle industry, these mergers cross national boundaries and globalize the structure of the industry. Roche's $11 billion acquisition of Germany's Boehringer Mannheim is an example of consolidation in the world's health care industry.

Roche's sales will now amount to $19 billion per year, based on medical diagnostics. Its acquisition of Boehringer Mannheim could push it past the world's current leader in diagnostics, Abbot Laboratories in the United States. It would also make Roche the sixth largest drug maker, with total sales in excess of $15 billion. Previously, Ciba-Geigy and Sandoz merged to form the world's largest drug company, Novartis. The result is that the industry is becoming dominated by a handful of giant companies.

This consolidation is driven by a change in strategic factors. Price is becoming an increasingly sensitive issue, as is the need to span continents and provide world products. New product development is also driving expanded product range as a strategic factor. There is a booming market for quick and simple tests for conditions ranging from pregnancy to cancer.

This case brings together two strategic options. In the first instance, we see Roche acquiring a competitor with a view to changing competitors' performance on strategic factors. With its consolidation, it hopes to become more competitive on price, product range and global availability, thus neutralizing any competitive advantage its competitors may have on these and other strategic factors.

Exercising another option, Roche has sold its orthopedic products maker, De Puy, to Johnson & Johnson, the world's fifth biggest drug maker, and decided to focus on drugs and diagnostics. In this way, not only is it exercising its Structure Strategy options but, through intensification, its options under Scope Strategy.

Let's now turn our attention to the fourth strategic option under Structure Strategy.

INNOVATION

When an organization produces an innovative product that makes current products in the marketplace obsolete, it alters competitors' performance on strategic factors. For instance, the credit card has had a major impact on the way cash is employed in purchases. Innovations such as this change the impact of strategic factors by simply overturning them.

In so doing, they effectively change competitors' performance on those same factors and neutralize any competitive advantage they may have had.

Innovation can be the means by which an organization establishes industry standards and thus ensures its long-term success. Companies that have done so and reaped considerable rewards include Computer Associates, Ericsson, Iomaga, Intel, Matsushita, Microsoft, Philips, Qualcom and Sony. These organizations all operate in industries where technological standards are important: consumer electronics, computer hardware and software, and telecommunications.

The competitive position of these organizations has been determined mainly because their technology became the dominant standard in the industry. The decline of Apple Computer can be attributed to its failure to establish its operating system as the industry standard for personal computers. Likewise, the success of Microsoft and Intel can be seen as driven by their ownership of the industry standard (the so-called Wintel standard).

Matsushita, of course, won a famous standards battle when its VHS videocassette recorder was adopted as the standard, over Sony's alternative Betamax format. Philips and Sony provided another example of success over competitors by jointly establishing their compact disc format as the standard for digital audio recordings.

Innovation alters competitors' performance on strategic factors by overturning them.

The classic example of an industry standard that, while innovative in its day, has locked an industry into acceptance of it is the QWERTY format of typewriter keyboards. Originally developed in the 1860s to reduce the tendency of type bars to clash and jam, it was designed to slow down typing speed. However, today, when type bars no longer exist, superior keyboard formats could be developed. Yet the QWERTY system remains dominant, and the important message here for innovation is that technological excellence is insufficient to guarantee success, once standards become established.

The main guideline in innovation and the establishment

of standards is to maximize the installed base. In other words, ensure that the innovation is adopted widely and locks out competitors. This can be done in a number of ways, including licensing and aggressive positioning of product and technology.

In all these cases, the effect of innovation has been to turn the reigning strategic factors of an industry on their head. They become irrelevant. Of course, the innovations and new industry standards must be protected.

Overturning strategic factors in an industry doesn't have to occur as a result of technological change, however. It can also occur through a change of thinking and a reconsideration of who the customers are in an industry. The case of Bright Horizons illustrates this.

BRIGHT HORIZONS

The child care industry has traditionally been seen as one that offers no barriers to entry, has low profit margins, is labour intensive, possesses no proprietary technology, offers few economies of scale, has little brand loyalty among customers and is subject to heavy regulation.

The circumstances would suggest: don't go there.

It's of interest, therefore, that Bright Horizons has become a successful company. It's done this through innovation.

Bright Horizons operates more than 340 child care centers in the United States, serving 40,000 children and employing 12,000 people. The business is both solid and profitable. It started in 1986, a time when child care in the United States was run like a commodity business. The emphasis was on low cost and hence low price to the customer, not on quality care. The result was an industry populated by organizations with high staff turnover.

So Bright Horizons saw an opportunity. It noticed that innovative companies like the children's shoe maker, Stride Rite, were establishing child care centers at the workplace and that these centers were of higher quality than the ones run by traditional child care chains. Bright Horizons got the idea that if it viewed employers rather than parents as the primary customer, it could establish partnering relationships with corporations and quickly gain access to a large number of working parents.

This is exactly what it did, and in so doing, identified the strategic factors relevant not only to its corporate customers, but to those customers' employees, the parents.

For its corporate customers, it identified risk as a strategic factor. It reduced that risk in corporations' eyes by securing insurance fifty times above the industry standard and by indemnifying those corporations. It also was able to show that by improving child care for their employees, these same corporations would reduce absenteeism and increase employee retention. As history would show, Chase Manhattan calculated that its center generated a 110% return on investment through reduced absenteeism.

Having addressed the strategic factors relevant to Bright Horizons' relationship with its primary customers, it could now turn its attention to the strategic factors relevant to its consumers, the parents of the children. Here the strategic factors included service quality, learning environment, center design and hours of operation. It then set about building competitive advantage on these and was successful.

Importantly, in a labour intensive industry such as child care, Bright Horizons recognized that its strategy for its customers (corporations) and consumers (parents) hinged upon a successful strategy for its own employees. In this case, we see not only the impact of innovation, but also the impact that key stakeholders have on each other. Bright Horizons set about becoming an employer of choice. It provided its teachers with salaries 20 to 30% above the industry average and offered comprehensive benefits, including health insurance, tuition reimbursement for the teachers' children if they used the child care centers, and a stimulating and innovative working environment.

Bright Horizons took a helicopter view of its industry. It recognised an opportunity to innovate and turn traditional strategic factors on their heads. It took a comprehensive view of the key stakeholders in its industry and set about developing competitive advantage at each of its links with them.[1]

SCALE, SCOPE AND STRUCTURE COMBINED

The next section provides an illustration of Scale, Scope and Structure Strategy for the customers of Reliance Trustee. This is not the real name of the company, but the example serves to illustrate how one organization used the whole range of strategic options covered in this and the previous chapters.

RELIANCE TRUSTEE

Reliance Trustee is a government-owned organization established to write wills and manage deceased estates. It has a number of private sector competitors. As part of government reform, Reliance Trustee was expected to become "commercial," i.e., to compete with the private sector and show a profit. Under these circumstances, it saw the following as being among its key strategic issues:

- Lack of directional focus; the need to crystallize the role of Reliance Trustee as compared to the private sector (community service obligations);

- The need to develop a professional self-image and an organizational one;

- Low commission rates for services.

The focus here, for purposes of illustration, is only on strategy with regard to the key stakeholder, *clients* – that is, those individuals who used the services of the organization.
The strategic factors for clients in the trustee industry are:

- Client service
- Reputation
- Price

- Security of funds
- Permanence of organization
- Service range.

Excerpts from this organization's strategic plan with respect to clients are listed below:

Scale Strategy
- Improve client service by:
  - establishing relationship marketing with current clients;
  - increasing speed of funds distribution and service delivery.
- Improve reputation by marketing the long-term and government-backed nature of the organization.
- Improve price choices by introducing a tailored fee structure (e.g. commercial versus non-commercial).
- Hold security of funds and permanence of organization by continuing current programs.
- Hold service range by continuing current range of services.

Scope Strategy
- Diversify into funds management for the general public.

Structure Strategy
- Lessen competitors' performance by:
  - establishing strategic alliances with lawyers;
  - lobbying government to permit Reliance Trustee to establish a Group Investment Fund;
  - lobbying government to allow Reliance Trustee to become co-executor of wills;
  - lobbying government to increase dollar values of situations where no court grants are necessary;
  - lobbying government to abolish requirement for power of attorney for private conveyancing.

In Scale Strategy, Reliance Trustee aims to lift its performance on certain strategic factors, while holding its performance on others. In doing so it wants to achieve competitive advantage for clients.

Scope Strategy involves a change in the nature of the organization's business: diversification into general funds management available to the general public — not just regular clients. Reliance Trustee has decided this after considering its ability to compete on a different set of strategic factors.

Reliance Trustee's response under Structure Strategy (to change competitors' performance on strategic factors) is interesting in that one of the options it intends to follow is to establish strategic alliances with lawyers, to cooperate with lawyers for mutual benefit. The other elements of its Structure Strategy involve lobbying the government to change the rules of the game. In this way the playing field would be more evenly balanced than it currently is, or even tilted in the direction of Reliance Trustee.

SEQUENCING STRATEGY DEVELOPMENT

There are two aspects to sequencing strategy development. The first is by key stakeholder. In other words, should you start with employees, with customers, with owners, with suppliers, and so on? The second aspect involves the development of Scale, Scope and Structure Strategy. For each of your key stakeholders, should you develop Scale Strategy before Scope and Structure, or vice versa?

Sequencing by Key Stakeholder

In the initial development of strategy, you need to focus on those key stakeholders who primarily influence the products or services of your organization or business unit. For example, a service organization such as a bank needs to focus initially on its customers and develop competitive advantage for them. Once this has been completed, the bank can then move on to consider the development of strategy for other key stakeholders.

It would be foolish to start with its employees if it had not first developed its strategy for its customers. For example, suppose a certain level of customer service and product range is seen as a key to obtaining competitive advantage. Not until that decision has been made, and that position taken, is the bank able to identify the skills it needs from employees. Certain employees may need to be attracted to the organization and others let go.

The development of strategy for customers may also impact on strategy development for suppliers. Having decided its position on customer service and product range, the bank may require a different relationship with its suppliers — perhaps a closer one with its supplier of information technology, for instance.

Strategy needs to be developed for the bank's owners, too, but again in the light of what was formulated for customers. Owners hold expectations, and the bank needs to operate on the relevant strategic factors to improve its competitiveness in owners' eyes. But it can only meet these expectations of dividends and capital growth if successful with customers.

Sequencing Scale, Scope and Structure Strategy

The first thing to note is that we apply Scale, Scope and Structure Strategy to each of our key stakeholders. All of them won't always be applicable; nonetheless, the strategic options in Figure 7.1 should be considered for each.

Because seeking competitive advantage through your existing activities is likely to be the most familiar route to your planning team and might be the most cost-effective, Scale Strategy seems a logical starting point. After this, the team will be in a position to consider diversifying or intensifying the organization's activities, while still, of course, seeking competitive advantage on strategic factors. Then, having considered Scope Strategy, team members can move their focus to Structure Strategy. The latter requires thinking of a different type, its aim being, as we know, to change competitors' performance on strategic factors.

Of course, while the Three S's of Strategy may be worked

through sequentially as indicated, your planning team will no doubt keep looking closely at the strategy it has already developed. It may change what was developed in earlier stages or alter previously espoused positions.

AN INTEGRATED APPROACH

Chapters 7, 8 and 9 have provided an integrated approach. In these chapters we've pulled together the six strategic options below and divided them into Scale, Scope and Structure Strategy:

- improve performance in present industry;
- diversity/intensify across industries;
- lobby rule makers and change industry rules (lobbying);
- link up with supplier, buyer or competitor (strategic alliance);
- acquire supplier, buyer or competitor (acquisition);
- develop a breakthrough approach (innovation).

The integration of these six seemingly disconnected strategic options is brought about by strategic factors, which underpin all six. In our System particular strategies are based on changing performance on strategic factors. If they aren't, they aren't strategies. (Refer to Figure 7.2, page 120 to refresh your memory on the difference between types, options and strategies.)

Tying these options together, as strategic factors do, makes the whole range more understandable. Otherwise, many people see no relationship between options such as acquisition, strategic alliance, improving performance and changing the scope of an organization.

This integrated approach also makes strategy more approachable. For many the idea of lobbying, for instance, seems out of their domain. Yet these chapters have shown that all options should be considered and, if appropriate, adopted.

Our integrated approach has also made strategy develop-

ment more accessible. We
suggest that planning teams
should approach strategy
design by considering *all*
three types of strategy and
the six strategic options they
provide. *Everyone* on a plan-
ning team can now think this way and develop specific
strategies based on strategic factors.

**Our integrated approach
makes strategy development
more understandable,
approachable and accessible.**

1   Brown, R., "How We Built a Strong Company in a Weak Industry," *Harvard
    Business Review*, 2001, February, 51-57.

CHAPTER 10

TRACKING STRATEGY IN REAL TIME

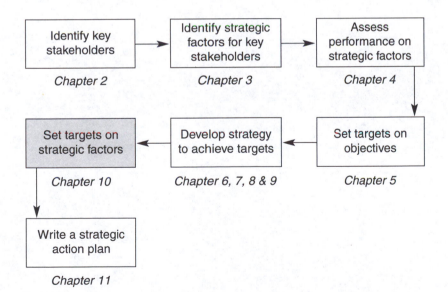

For most organizations the task of tracking strategy is almost impossible. Sure, they know by undertaking a *group* of strategies, *some* results will follow, but they have never, until now, been able to link individual strategies to specific objectives.

This book has shown how to do that — to link employee strategies to employee objectives, such as improved productivity and increased innovation. Or, how to link customer strategies to customer objectives such as increased revenue.

In this chapter we'd like to go further.

Wouldn't it be great if, in addition to tracking strategies against objectives, you could track the strategies themselves in real time? You see, tracking strategy against objectives involves a lag in time. For example, let us say we improve customer service in a Hilton Hotel. Our objectives have been to increase revenue from current customers by having them return and to increase the number of customers overall. The latter occurs when our current customers tell potential customers to stay at our hotel.

But there's a lag here, a delayed reaction. It may be weeks or months before the hotel's revenue stream improves as a consequence of the improvement in customer service. Shouldn't we also be tracking performance on customer service as well?

Here's where strategic factors re-emerge. We can use them to monitor how strategy has been implemented, *and* we can use them as leading indicators of results on objectives.

The concept of a leading indicator is simple. One indicator (measure) becomes a leading indicator of another if it predicts results on the latter. In our hotel example, measures of customer service (among others) predict results on measures of revenue increase and, as such, are leading indicators. Measures of strategic factors become leading indicators of performance on objectives.

Measures of strategic factors become leading indicators of performance on objectives.

Using this method will assist you greatly to monitor and predict your success.

LEADING INDICATORS BASED ON STRATEGIC FACTORS

Let's look back at Figure 5.4, on page 79. Here we see objectives illustrated as arrows going from the key stakeholders to the organization. From Chapter 5 we now understand what these arrows mean and how to develop effective objectives. We also understand how to develop key performance indicators (KPI's) on those objectives and set targets on the KPI's.

Strategic factors provide the ideal source of leading indicators.

What we want to do now is to see what use can be made of the arrows that travel in the opposite direction. These arrows are shown as strategic factors for customers, for employees, for suppliers and for owners.

So what do we have so far? We have KPI's that are based on objectives and targets set on these KPI's. We have strategy set on strategic factors that has been developed to achieve these targets. It makes complete sense. But what if we could develop measures on the strategic factors themselves? What would this tell us about the performance of an organization or business unit?

STEPS TO TRACKING STRATEGY IN REAL TIME

To track strategy in real time you need to follow these steps:

1. Focus on the strategic factors affected by your strategy

2. Define them

3. Develop measures on them

4. Reduce the list of measures to develop key performance indicators (KPI's)

5. Set targets on KPI's

Step One

FOCUSING ON STRATEGIC FACTORS

You may or may not wish to monitor your organization's performance on *all* the strategic factors relevant to a key stakeholder. This may be because not all of them have been impacted by your strategy.

Take for example, Middleton Timber, which we've already encountered in Chapter 4. The strategic factors for its *customers,* the builders and owner/builders, are:

- Range of products
- Product quality (consistency)
- Customer service
- Delivery
- Price and trade terms

Assessment of its performance with customers suggests that the company needs to focus on a narrower range of builders, cutting back on its *range of products.* It believes that competitive advantage will also be achieved by improving its performance on *product quality.* And it aims to lift its performance on *delivery,* to become an industry benchmark. Finally, it is looking to raise its *price* for this narrower range of customers, who appreciate high quality product and delivery that is second to none.

From this description of Middleton Timber's strategy, we can see two ways of tracking its performance. The first is by tracking results on its objective "to increase revenue from customers." Middleton Timber hopes that by improving its performance on the strategic factors identified in its strategy, it will increase its existing customers' purchases, attract additional customers and increase revenue.

A second route it can take to monitor performance involves tracking the strategic factors identified *in* its strategy: range of products, product quality, delivery and price. So this second route entails developing key performance indicators and targets on these strategic factors.

Step Two

DEFINING STRATEGIC FACTORS

We cannot stress enough the importance of the second step. If you produce clear definitions of your strategic factors, the measures will drop out easily. If, on the other hand, you attempt to develop measures without clear definitions, you and your team will struggle.

Without clear definitions of strategic factors, your team will struggle.

Let's now look at how we might develop definitions of the strategic factors relevant to your organization's key stakeholders.

There are at least three sources of definitions:

1. You can look around at how other organizations define strategic factors, e.g., product quality.

2. You can, with your planning team, develop a definition of what you think a key stakeholder might mean by a strategic factor, e.g., customer service.

3. You can ask your key stakeholders themselves for their definition of a strategic factor, e.g., range of products.

All three have their place. But a problem arises if you only depend on the first two sources and do not employ the third. What are the dangers here? That the definitions may be completely at odds with what is appropriate for your organization or business unit. For example, product quality in the timber products industry is quite different from product quality in the health care industry. So while you can learn from the way in which strategic factors are defined in other industries, you would be unwise to adopt their definitions without scrutinizing them intensely. Unwise adoption has distorted organizations' measures in very serious ways.

Of course, at the end of the day, it's up to a planning team to decide which definitions are appropriate. So the second source of definitions above *must* come into play at some point. This is so whether the strategic factors are for customers, employees, suppliers, owners or any other key stakeholder.

Much discussion occurs in planning sessions as to what is meant by a strategic factor. Customer service is a good example. Your team may spend a lot of time discussing what it means in your industry. However, it doesn't matter how your team defines customer service if that definition is at odds with how *customers* define it. Yet, again and again, you'll find organizations and business units developing detailed definitions of strategic factors without reference to how their key stakeholders define them.

> **Again and again, you'll find organizations developing definitions of strategic factors without reference to how their key stakeholders define them.**

It is for these reasons that you must be sure to employ the third source above: be certain that the definitions you use are those that your relevant key stakeholder uses. Bear in mind the five methods given previously for identifying strategic factors in Chapter 4:

- Customer responses to performance
  (e.g., letters, phone calls, conversations)

- Sales force feedback
  (e.g., sales reports on product/service sales)

- Customer survey
  (e.g., questionnaire or interviews)

- Customer focus groups
  (i.e., small-group, in-depth discussions)

- Competitor activity
  (e.g., changes in their performance)

Step Three

DEVELOPING MEASURES ON STRATEGIC FACTORS

The fundamental way to obtain clear definitions of strategic factors and develop measures on those factors is by interviewing your key stakeholders.

To illustrate, consider the example of how we developed measures on the strategic factors applicable to the customers of a company we'll call Wakefield.

WAKEFIELD

Wakefield distributes gift products to retail stores, like shopping center gift shops. It has been increasingly buffeted by competition and it's interesting to take note of its key strategic issues before considering how it developed measures on strategic factors. These issues are:

- Change to distribution system
- Overseas opportunities for growth
- Defining the core competencies of the organization
- Acquisition and new product development
- Exposure to seasonality/trends in sales
- Branding of products

We, their consultants, interviewed the owners of a sample of sixteen retail stores to identify the strategic factors relevant to them. The results were:

- Price and margin
- Product range
- Customer service
- Delivery
- Packaging/presentation

What do each of these mean? From its knowledge of the industry, Wakefield's planning team would be able to develop definitions of these factors. We would, too. *But the important definitions are those that come from the retailers them-*

selves. So, asking the retailers is precisely what we did.

But we didn't stop there. Based on the definitions they gave, we next asked how they would suggest measuring each of them. A very rich amount of information was gathered. To illustrate, let's take one of the strategic factors and provide the retailers' definition of it. The factor is price and margin, and it had six components:

- Dollar price
- Retail price minus purchase price
- Trading terms
- Discounts
- Returns or exchanges
- Consistency of pricing

Immediately we can see the richness of this definition. Retailers are concerned about price points, hence "dollar price" above. They know that the price should not exceed certain ranges appropriate to their stores, as this would impede their ability to sell the product. They are also concerned about price because it will affect turnover. So while margin is important, a low-margin, high-volume product will beat a high-margin product that hardly ever sells.

The definition is also concerned with trading terms, i.e., when retailers have to pay, as this affects the profitability of the transactions between them and Wakefield. Discounts for volume are another relevant point: they increase the margin available to retailers. Wakefield's policy on returns or exchanges also affects margin. And finally, the consistency of the price is important because customers dislike fluctuations.

The retailers then provided clear measures for the strategic factor price and margin based on the definition above.

Step Four

DEVELOPING KEY PERFORMANCE INDICATORS ON STRATEGIC FACTORS

It is certainly obvious how important it is to get "inside the head" of your key stakeholders. Once you do, you see the world from their perspective. You're then in a much better position to develop relevant definitions and measures. The example below lists KPI's for the strategic factors for farmers of Griffith Irrigation, an actual organization which we assisted with planning and measurement, although its name has been changed.

GRIFFITH IRRIGATION

Griffith Irrigation is government-owned and a natural monopoly. This means that when it comes to the supply of water to farmers in this region, there is little competition. Griffith Irrigation takes water from nearby rivers and distributes it via large canals. From these large canals, narrow channels run alongside farmers' properties. Griffith Irrigation staff open gates on the channels and let the water flood on to farmers' properties. There are meters on the gates that measure the amount of water each farm receives.

The strategic factors for farmers are:

- Customer service
- Water quality
- Water prices

Customer service is defined as the extent to which water orders are filled on time. This means that Griffith Irrigation staff have to open the gate that leads to a farmer's property on the date he ordered, and close that gate when the ordered quantity of water has been discharged onto the farm. *Water quality* is defined as the extent to which water meets certain criteria. It is analyzed for contaminants, such as pesticides and salts, and for the existence of grass seeds. *Water prices* are a positive factor if they are seen to be fair in relation to the service rendered. These factors and abbreviated versions of these definitions are shown in Figure 10.1.

Figure 10.1   **KPI's on Strategic Factors for Farmers**

Strategic Factor	Definition	KPI
Customer Service	Getting water orders on time to customers	• % of water orders on time • % of farmers satisfied with service
Water Quality	Physical and chemical tests of water to meet standard	• % of quality test results between receivals and discharges that meet standard • % of farmers satisfied with water quality
Water Prices	Price/megaliter of water delivered to farm	• $ total operations and maintenance costs • % rating on price compared to comparable irrigation organizations

These strategic factors came to the fore in actual interviews with the farmers, who also supplied the definitions and nominated the measures that would be appropriate for each Strategic Factor.

Note the column "KPI" (key performance indicator). We've moved from defining and collecting "measures" from farmers, to developing KPI's. In the step sequence, we've come to Step 4: *Reduce the list of measures to develop key performance indicators (KPI's)*. Figure 10.1 shows the results of this reduction.

In the table customer service is defined as "getting water orders on time to customers." This is measured by two KPI's: "% of water orders on time," and "% of farmers satisfied with service." Both objective and subjective measures are brought together here. The objective measure "% of water orders on time" is supplemented by a subjective measure based on farmers' *perception* of customer service.

Water quality is defined as "physical and chemical tests of water to meet standard." Again there are two KPI's relevant to that definition. The first is "% of quality tests between receivals and discharges that meet standard." Results on this measure are derived from the chemical and physical testing of the water between the time it is taken from rivers to the time it is discharged onto farms. Testing involves detecting chemicals in the water or weed seeds and other contaminants. The second KPI for water quality is subjective, based on the farmers' perception of water quality.

"Water prices" simply refers to the price of water delivered to the farm. It is measured by two measures, one of which requires some explanation. The first measure is "$ total operations and maintenance costs," while the second is "% rating on price compared to comparable irrigation organizations." On the surface, it may seem odd to have a measure of "prices" in terms of "costs." However, we need to understand the way in which prices are established by Griffith Irrigation.

The price per megaliter of water is set by taking the total costs for the organization, adding a margin and dividing it by the megaliters used. The price of water is therefore firmly linked to total operations and maintenance costs. This situation arises because Griffith Irrigation is a cost-recovery entity and government-owned. It needs to keep its costs down in order to keep its prices competitive. To assess whether its prices are competitive, Griffith Irrigation has also developed a KPI that rates its price compared to similar irrigation organizations.

As one of its objectives, Griffith Irrigation seeks to grow revenue. To do this, it has to do well on the strategic factors relevant to farmers: customer service, water quality and water prices. Farmers will then stay with this particular organization and not seek to substitute its method of irrigation with alternative technology. If it falls down on these strategic factors, the farmers will start looking for other ways of obtaining water for their crops. The result will, of course, be a decline in revenue for Griffith Irrigation.

It is clear from this example how, by measuring perform-ance on the strategic factors for farmers, we are able to predict future revenue. Thus KPI's on "customer service," "water quality" and "water prices" become *leading indicators* of the KPI "$ revenue from farmers."

Step Five

SETTING TARGETS ON KPI'S

Figure 10.2 contains the strategic factors and the KPI's from Figure 10.1. The definitions from the latter have been deleted and a column called "Target" has been added. If you run your eye down that column, you'll see how specific quanti-ties have been set for the KPI's in the adjacent column. For example, for the KPI "% of water orders on time," two targets have been set: "90% in 2 days" and "100% in 4 days." There are at least four influences that come to bear in estab-lishing targets like that, as Figure 10.3 illustrates.

One influence shown in Figure 10.3 is *performance last period*. For example, the target on water quality in Figure 10.2, "more than 90% of our farmers rate our water quality highly suitable for irrigation" was set by looking at the pre-vious satisfaction level, which was less than 90%. The target of 90% reflects the desire to improve performance on this Strategic Factor of water quality.

A second influence is *imperatives*. Often these are finan-cial, such as a return on shareholders' funds, but they don't have to be. In the case of Griffith Irrigation, Figure 10.2 high-lights the absolute need to fill water orders; if they aren't filled, crops die and the very existence of the authority is threatened. This certainly sounds like an imperative! So the targets "90% in 2 days" and "100% in 4 days" come about because water simply has to be delivered.

A third influence on target setting is *benchmarking*, which involves comparing one organization with another best-practice organization in order to equal its performance and, if possible, exceed it. This aim has led Griffith Irrigation to establish the target, "top 10% of comparable irrigators" on

Figure 10.2   **Targets on KPI's**

Strategic Factor	KPI	Target
Customer Service	• % of water orders on time	• 90% in 2 days; 100% in 4 days
	• % of farmers satisfied with service	• More than 70% of customers rate our service "very good" on annual survey
Water Quality	• % of quality test results between receivals and discharges that meet standard	• 100%
	• % of farmers satisfied with water quality	• More than 90% of our farmers rate our water quality "highly suitable for irrigation"
Water Prices	• $ total operations and maintenance costs	• $250 million
	• % rating on price compared to comparable irrigation organizations	• Top 10% of comparable irrigators

Figure 10.3   **Target-Setting Influences**

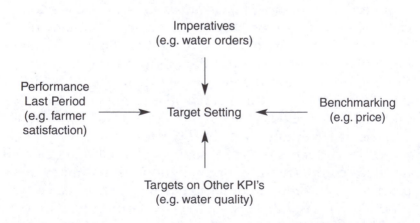

the strategic factor of water prices. Its aim is to be competitive on price to such an extent that it places itself in the top 10% of irrigation organizations.

Staying with Figure 10.3, we note that a fourth influence on target setting is *targets on other KPI's*. In other words, targets are set on one KPI through knowledge of targets on another. There is a cause-and-effect relationship and in the next section we cover this in detail. This aspect of target setting is new and, in dealing with it, we're at the leading edge in this field.

OBJECTIVES, STRATEGIC FACTORS, AND CAUSE AND EFFECT

We've seen from the example of Griffith Irrigation how objectives can be set for a *particular key stakeholder*, strategy written and performance on strategic factors monitored. We've seen these linkages for one key stakeholder — farmers. There are also linkages *between* key stakeholders, so that, in the case of Griffith Irrigation, results for employees, for example, drive results for suppliers, farmers and other key stakeholders.

This is an exciting idea, another way to track strategy: through linkages between key stakeholders.

This is an exciting idea, *another way to track strategy:* through linkages between key stakeholders. Figure 10.4 illustrates this graphically.

We see here how strategic factors and objectives are linked for a single key stakeholder (e.g. employees) and how objectives for one key stakeholder are linked to strategic factors for another key stakeholder. Our System has been employed in an innovative way: to look at cause and effect between KPI's for different key stakeholders.

Let's read the Figure from left to right, starting with employees. Strategy for them drives KPI's on strategic factors, e.g., % rating against reward system benchmark (1). In turn, the KPI's on strategic factors drives the KPI's on

Figure 10.4 Cause and Effect Between Objectives and Strategic Factors

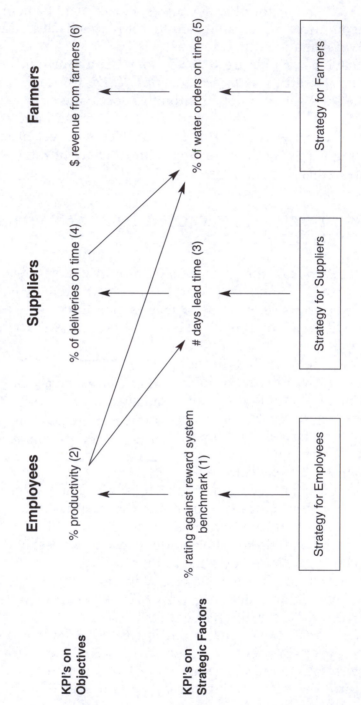

objectives, e.g., % productivity (2). So, for Griffith Irrigation to track the success of its employee strategy, it can check its effect on KPI's on strategic factors as well as its impact on KPI's on objectives.

But there's a flow-on effect from this strategy, as we see illustrated by the arrows moving out from KPI's on objectives. Performance on these affect the KPI's on strategic factors for farmers and for suppliers. So the success of Griffith Irrigation's employee strategy is evident in the KPI's on strategic factors and objectives for employees, as well as in KPI's throughout the model.

Figure 10.4 illustrates how supplier strategy, too, can be tracked, just to give another example. It can be done directly on the KPI's applicable to suppliers, but it can also be done on those for farmers. To reiterate, the impact of strategy can be detected by impact on other key stakeholders.

While cause and effect in the Figure move from left to right, targets are set from right to left. We see this in Figure 10.5. Suppose, for example, Griffith Irrigation has set a target to increase revenue from farmers by $25 million. With the implications of that flowing from right to left, it's clear that the target, which is based on the KPI "$ revenue from farmers" (6), impacts on targets for the KPI's on strategic factors for farmers. Here the KPI is "% of water orders on time" (5).

The target set on this KPI then affects targets established on KPI's on objectives for suppliers, such as "% of deliveries on time" (4); and KPI's on objectives for employees, such as "% productivity" (2). These and other linkages are illustrated by the arrows in Figure 10.5.

So it is that knowledge of the cause and effect between strategy for one key stakeholder and that for others leads to a way of linking the targets for the former with those for the others. We've seen a *remarkable way to track strategy* - both in real time, via the immediately impacted strategic factor, and in a delayed way as shown in the model in Figure 10.4.

Figure 10.5 **Setting Targets**

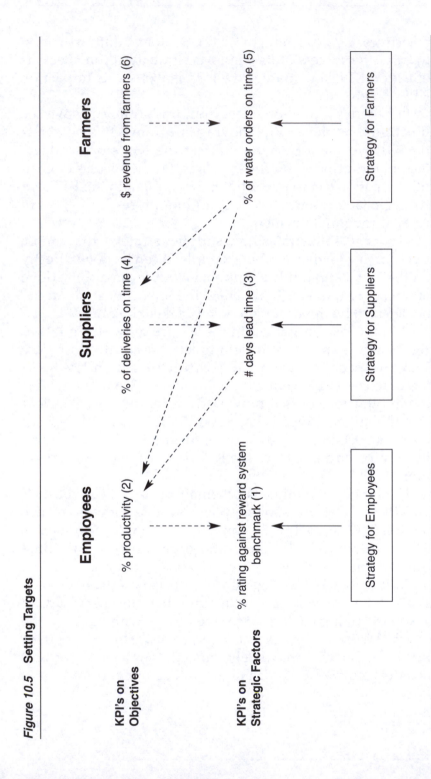

SEARS ROEBUCK

Sears Roebuck makes an interesting example for two reasons.

The first of these is that the company links results for its key stakeholders. It links results for its employees to results for its customers and results for its investors. Performance measures are classified accordingly.

The second reason the example is interesting is that Sears rejected the balanced scorecard with its four pre-set categories: customer perspective, financial perspective, internal business process perspective, and innovation and learning perspective. As the company wrote, "We wanted to go well beyond the usual balanced scorecard — commonly just a set of untested assumptions — and nail down the drivers of future financial performance with statistical rigor."[1]

The Sears story is more than one of strategy. Its people developed what they called the Employee-Customer-Profit Chain and it produces Total Performance Indicators or TPI's (KPI's in our model), which show how well they are performing with their key stakeholders: customers, employees and investors. Via the Employee-Customer-Profit Chain, a cause-and-effect relationship is shown to exist between employee behavior, customer behavior, and results for investors.

The Sears people also sought to supplement the usual financial measures with non-financial ones. Importantly, they wanted these latter to be every bit as rigorous and auditable.

In effect, Sears links its strategy for employees to its strategy for customers to its strategy for shareholders. It is also able to demonstrate to employees how effective performance by them leads to effective performance for customers and for Sears' investors.

Sears believes that this approach gives the company a competitive advantage and, indeed, the results are impressive. Independent surveys had shown that national customer satisfaction in retailing had fallen for several consecutive years. Sears, however, went against this trend. Since the system was introduced, employee satisfaction at the company has risen, as has customer satisfaction. When Sears translates these improvements through their model, the four per cent improvement in customer satisfaction translates into more than $200 million in additional revenue over the twelve-month period in which improvements were made. With its current after-tax margin and price-earnings ratio, this increase in revenue translates into an increase in their market capitalization of nearly $250 million.

This example pulls together a number of points from this chapter. The first is that Sears rejected the balanced score-card with its four pre-set categories as "a set of untested assumptions." Instead, it thought through the relationships that it had with its key stakeholders: employees, customers and investors. It then set about linking outcomes for employees to outcomes for customers to outcomes for investors, developed key performance indicators (Total Performance Indicators in their system) for each of their key stakeholders, and looked for links between them via a cause-and-effect model.

The third point of note relevant to this chapter is that, by developing this cause-and-effect model, Sears was able to see how improvements for one key stakeholder impacted on others and, thus, where they needed to develop strategy. They could decide how many resources should be applied to raising results for employees and customers and how this might flow on to improved results for investors.

While Sears don't employ objectives and strategic factors as we define them in our System, they nonetheless provide an interesting and useful illustration of connecting key stakeholders and key performance indicators in order to track the success of an organization's strategy.

STRATEGY FOR *ALL* KEY STAKEHOLDERS

This book started by stressing the importance of identifying the *key* stakeholders of an organization or business unit. We've kept this theme constant throughout the chapters. In this chapter and especially in Figure 10.4, its importance is obvious. Strategy for one affects strategy for others.

There is a *dependence* between key stakeholders, and recognizing it is essential in developing strategy and tracking its success. To develop strategy for only one key stakeholder and take the others for granted is to invite failure. Yet this is precisely what is happening when organizations concentrate only on the requirements of their shareholders

> **There is a dependence between key stakeholders, and recognising it is essential in developing strategy and tracking its success.**

and ignore the needs of customers, or focus on customers and overlook the needs of their employees, or concentrate on customers and employees and take suppliers for granted.

Our Strategic Factor System recognizes the interdependence of key stakeholders, anticipates their needs, and develops strategy for them. As can be seen in this chapter, it also enables the tracking of strategy in real time and assists in tracing its impact on an organization's or business unit's key stakeholders.

If you'd like assistance in developing and linking your key performance indicators for your organization or business unit, our company Strategic Factors has developed software that not only takes you through the process, but helps you to investigate cause-and-effect relationships between KPI's. If you want to take this further and link several business units throughout your organization, we have software that facilitates this task. Information on these products is available through our website *www.strategicfactors.com*

How to ensure that strategy gets acted upon and is implemented effectively is the subject of the next chapter.

---

1   Rucci, A.J., Kirn, S.P. and Quinn, R.T., "The Employee-Customer-Profit Chain at Sears," *Harvard Business Review*, 1998, January-February, 82-97.

CHAPTER 11

THE NEED FOR ACTION

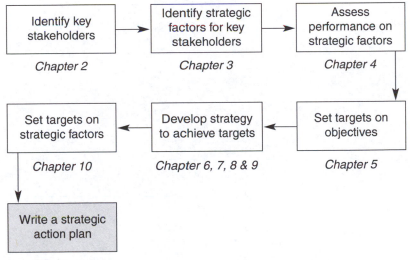

Lack of implementation has been one of the major failings in strategic planning. Our company has visited numerous organizations whose strategic plans gather dust rather than results.

There are many reasons for this situation, but a major one lies in the design of the plan itself. As a document, a strategic plan has to have certain components if it is to be capable of implementation. And most plans lack these components. How, for instance, can vague statements concerning mission, vision and values be implemented unless these are translated into specifics? Unfortunately, many strategic plans are populated by platitudes and fail to connect with actual programs and projects.

> **Lack of implementation has been one of the major failings in strategic planning.**

So, for many organizations, it isn't lack of motivation on the part of managers and staff or faulty organizational systems that hold back implementation — it's the plan's design. What it means for *individual action* simply isn't clear.

In fact, in some strategic plans, the action component is missing entirely.

The purpose of this chapter is to discuss seven common mistakes in strategic planning and provide remedies for them (Figure 11.1). The chapter also pulls together many of the book's themes with special attention to the importance of action planning.

Mistake One

FAILURE TO SPELL OUT COMPETITIVE ADVANTAGE

It is through strategic planning that we seek to find avenues whereby we can win and be successful. This implies having a competitive advantage over our competitors to such an extent that customers and other key stakeholders choose our organization in preference to others. Failure to spell out competitive advantage nullifies strategic planning's intent.

Figure 11.1 **Strategic Plan Faults and Remedies**

Faults	Remedies
• Failure to spell out competitive advantage	• Instruct managers on what "competitive advantage" is • Have planning team focus on the purpose of a strategic plan – producing a winning formula
• Basing plans on superficial analysis	• Instruct managers in "industry and performance analysis" • Instruct managers to think strategically
• Plans become "wish lists" rather than action-oriented documents	• Go beyond "mission," "vision" and "values" in planning • Document key stakeholders and the strategic factors relevant to each stakeholder • Develop an action plan as part of the strategic plan
• Getting caught up in operational issues	• Segregate issues into "strategic" and "operational" • Bring operational issues back on line after strategic issues have been addressed
• Plans take the form of budgets with some "window dressing"	• Put aside financial and accounting considerations in the early stages of planning • Employ methods that focus upon industry trends, competitor activity and customers' tastes and preferences
• Planning becomes a form-filling exercise	• Give guidance but avoid "straightjacket" • Within guidelines encourage individuality, innovation and risk-taking
• Plans become unfocused "to do" lists	• Have planning team reflect upon planning assumptions • Employ techniques that have managers think beyond solving operational problems

Remedy: Managers need to be instructed on the concept of competitive advantage: doing something better than someone else in the eyes of a key stakeholder. For example, an organization may have a competitive advantage in customer service because it delivers more promptly and more reliably than a competitor. This difference in performance is valued by customers, who constitute a key stakeholder.

Two things are important here and were discussed extensively in Chapters 6, 7, 8 and 9. First, the competitive advantage is defined by the key stakeholder. If, for example, the latter were not interested in such an improvement in customer service, it would not be a competitive advantage. The other thing that is important is not to mistake internal capabilities for competitive advantage. An organization may have a

Managers need to be instructed on the concept of competitive advantage.

better information system and a more advanced computer than one of its competitors, but this is not in itself a competitive advantage. Customers do not buy an organization's better computer or its better information system. They buy what such systems produce. A more advanced computer and a better information system may provide the potential for a competitive advantage, but unless this is translated into something an external stakeholder values, there is no advantage.

Mistake Two

BASING PLANS ON SUPERFICIAL ANALYSIS

Strategic planning must avoid "shooting from the hip." At the other extreme, however, it must avoid "paralysis by analysis." What is needed here is a balance between the two extremes. The analysis needs to be at a level that is appropriate for a strategic understanding of an organization's future. It should not be overwhelmed by historical accounting data. It should analyze the present players as well as the trends and changes occurring in an industry. Lack of such analysis can only lead to crass decision-making.

Remedy: Our company invites organizations to undertake both industry analysis and performance analysis. Under the first we look at industry changes and trends, how value is built up in the industry (the value chain), how the industry is segmented and how attractive these segments are. Such analysis is far from superficial, and while it forces managers to think deeply about their industry, it avoids making analysis an end in itself.

Next comes performance analysis, the subject of Chapter 4. This is not accounting or financial performance. This is strategic performance based on how an organization has performed in comparison to its industry competitors. It involves assessing organizational performance on the strategic factors pertinent to the industry — factors such as product quality, customer service and price. It is quite remarkable how planning teams discover through this analysis that they have blind spots concerning the industry, major differences of opinion about it and a real lack of sufficient information to make appropriate strategic decisions.

Mistake Three

PLANS BECOME "WISH LISTS" RATHER THAN ACTION-ORIENTED DOCUMENTS

Many strategic plans remain as pious hopes that something will change. They become, in effect, just "wish lists." They are "snuffed out" at the point of writing down mission, vision, goals and other non-specific, non-quantified and non-action-oriented statements. Nothing really changes in the organization.

The fault here lies in not understanding what a strategic plan is supposed to do: change the decision-making, and make the organization successful.

Remedy: Have the planning team examine the key stakeholders that impact on performance and gain a grasp of the nature of the transactions that occur between these key stakeholders and the organization (Chapters 2 and 3). The emphasizing of one (or a few) of the factors that lie within these transactions, for each key stakeholder, gives the organization a competitive advantage. Such strategic factors may be concerned with, for example, product quality, customer service or product range.

Another part of the method to avoid wish lists involves the addition of a simple device: an *action plan*. An action plan states what is to be done, who is to do it and when it is to be completed (who, what and when). It is the tool that triggers the implementation of strategy. When a team goes to this extent in its strategic planning, they start to drive the decisions that people take.

An action plan is the tool that triggers the implementation of strategy.

The position of an action plan is illustrated in the Strategy Development Funnel, back on page 73. This figure shows that action planning follows the development of strategy and deals with its implementation. But it must be integral to the strategic plan itself.

An action plan is a simple but important component of any successful strategic plan. It's the part of the exercise that goes most smoothly. Members of planning teams find the concrete and specific nature of action-planning a relief, following on the heels of the rather nebulous and future-looking work involved in developing strategy. So don't hesitate to go that extra step and develop an action plan. You'll reap considerable rewards.

Illustrated in Figure 11.2 is an action plan for the strategy "improve customer service by making service more personal and better focused." This strategy aims to give competitive advantage on the strategic factor of customer service.

Were this organization to walk away from its strategic planning exercise with statements of strategy but no action plan, you know the consequences. Little would be done and, after several months, those involved in the exercise would

Figure 11.2   **Action Plan for Strategy**

Strategy	Action	Responsibility	Completion Date
• Improve customer service by making service more personal and better focused	• Personalise customer service at head office by having nominated persons deal with certain accounts exclusively	Customer Service Manager	30 April, 20XX
	• Run product information nights to allow customers to view new products properly displayed	National Sales Manager	14 June, 20XX
	• Conduct a series of customer service workshops for internal staff, especially focusing on the problems in accounts and returns	Human Resources Manager	11 May, 20XX
	• Improve systems in accounts and returns to eliminate customer problems	Credit Manager	25 March, 20XX

be disillusioned.

In Figure 11.2, a statement of strategy has been translated into specific actions for designated individuals to complete by certain dates. Supplied is a sample of only four such actions, but this organization, an importer of gift products, had actually identified many more. Various members of the company become involved. In the "Responsibility" column, you see Customer Service Manager, National Sales Manager, Human Resources Manager and Credit Manager.

Note also in the "Action" column how the strategy has been broken down into component actions. For example, nominated persons are to deal with certain accounts. The gift importer's customers were retail stores, not individuals. In the second action, the customer service is to be improved by running product information nights for customers, i.e. retail stores. In the third action, a series of workshops is to be conducted for internal staff to address problems in accounts and returns. And in the fourth action, systems in accounts and returns are to be improved and problems the stores are having are to be eliminated.

As a result of these actions, further actions will most likely be required. It isn't as though on 14th June, 20XX all action to improve customer service will cease.

Let me urge you again to write a good action plan and make it an integral part of your strategic plan. It will ensure that your organization's strategy is implemented. It isn't that hard, and it *is* essential.

Mistake Four

GETTING CAUGHT UP IN OPERATIONAL ISSUES

Issues can be categorised as "strategic" or "operational." *Strategic* issues are concerned with where an organization is heading and with its competitiveness. *Operational* issues, on the other hand, are concerned with efficiency. Many "strategic plans" fail to rise above the operational. They fail to see the strategic issues on the horizon, because they are too grounded in the present.

Operational issues to do with cash flows, complaints, staff allocation and the like are the day-to-day affairs of any manager. These issues occupy 90% of most managers' time. For this reason, they often dominate strategic planning sessions, too.

Remedy: The way out of this is to segregate issues into "strategic" or "operational." The planning team needs to put the latter to one side for the time being and concentrate on dealing with strategic issues. (Examples of key strategic issues were provided in chapter 4.) Having done this, and decided where the organization is heading, it can then turn its attention to the operational issues and see which of these might become impediments to the implementation of the new strategic direction.

For example, let us suppose one of the operational issues is that the organization has a poor organization structure. While this can be put aside initially in the planning meeting while strategic issues are considered, it must come back on line to be dealt with later in the session. If this is not done, the organization's structure may act as an impediment to dealing with the issues.

Mistake Five

PLANS TAKE THE FORM OF BUDGETS WITH SOME "WINDOW-DRESSING"

Lip service is often paid to strategic planning. Management says it should have it. However, what is often produced is the same old budget with a few pages added at the front and re-titled a "strategic plan." The window dressing is the few pages attached to the traditional budget, as no thorough strategic analysis has been undertaken.

This situation occurs because many managers do not appreciate the importance of a strategic plan to an organization. They will comply externally with what senior management says should be done, going along with the drawing up of a strategic plan, but their heart is not in the job. Many of them think it is a waste of time, "only words." What they prefer to concentrate on is the hard data in the budget.

Keep going with this way of thinking and strategic planning becomes a farce.

Remedy: The way to prevent window dressing is to put aside financial considerations in the early stages of the planning process. Managers need to be able to "kick back their chairs" and do some "crystal ball-gazing" before attempting to put numbers to their considerations. They need to ask: Where is the industry heading? What are competitors up to? How are the tastes and preferences of customers changing? etc. These questions must be asked before any attempt is made to quantify strategy in dollar terms.

On the other hand, it is extremely important that strategies are eventually quantified and their impact on the organization considered and measured. This was the focus of Chapters 5 and 10.

Put aside financial considerations in the early stages of the planning process.

Mistake Six

PLANNING BECOMES A FORM-FILLING EXERCISE

In large organizations there is often an attempt to ensure that uniformity exists between the various business units whose task it is to complete a strategic plan. This uniformity can lead to what amounts to a "form-filling exercise" because standardization is pushed to an extreme; managers "go through the motions" with a centrally-designed form.

The problem with this approach is that it drives out initiative and fresh, original thinking. While some guidelines are required, once strategic planning becomes purely a routine activity, it has lost its significance.

Remedy: Managers in large organizations should receive guidance on how to prepare a strategic plan for their business units. A format should be suggested: a table of contents, a description of what each part of the document projects and an appropriate length. If an organization goes much further beyond these guidelines, it runs the risk of designing a straightjacket for its managers.

In the past some organizations have so formalized strategic planning that all managers needed to do was fill in the blank spaces, tick the appropriate boxes, list the alternatives that were rejected and then move on! What is evident in these instances is that little thought was given to the planning process and few people were involved.

The bottom line is that appropriate guidelines need to be set, but a manager's freedom to be innovative must not be curtailed.

Mistake Seven

PLANS BECOME UNFOCUSED "TO DO" LISTS

Very often people who are called together to develop strategic plans are impatient to get the job done. At 9 o'clock on the first day of the planning exercise, they cannot wait to get down to what needs doing. The result is a strategic plan that is full of action, but lacks coherent thought and direction. There are many things to do, but there is no focus on what this action adds up to. (The unfocused "to do" list lies at the opposite extreme to the "wish list.")

Remedy: The way to avoid this fault is to hold people back from writing down, as soon as they meet, all the things they want to have changed. Instead, have them reflect on their industry and any assumptions they might be making about the future. Slowing the team down by having them analyze their situations, write scenarios of what their industry might be like in five years' time and similar techniques provided in Chapter 4 gives the planning team a breathing space before plunging into the actions necessary to make the organization competitive.

ACTION IS KEY

This chapter has been concerned with strategic plan mistakes and their remedies. They're well worth addressing since, if you don't, your chances of success are slim.

In our consulting work we see most all of these mistakes. We see organizations whose managers don't understand what competitive advantage is. We see organizations developing strategy without the appropriate analysis. We see strategic plans which are merely wish lists and lack an action component or ones that are operational plans retitled. We see organizations calling budgets with a cover sheet, "Strategic Plans." We see still other organizations standardising plans to the point that they are just form-filling exercises. At the other extreme, we see plans that are full of actions but lack purpose.

To avoid these faults, follow the remedies summarised in Figure 11.1.

Why not use the list of faults as a check list now? How many of the seven faults do you have in your strategic plan? How many of the fifteen remedies should you be implementing?

And there's that word again — *implementation*. It's been particularly stressed in this chapter as it's often overlooked in strategic planning.

Remember, strategy without action is dead.

Remember, strategy without action is dead.

CHAPTER 12

OUTSIDE LOOKING IN

This book commenced with an observation we know to be true because we have often seen it verified.

The observation is that it is difficult for us to see our organizations and business units from the outside in. It's not easy to comprehend *outcomes* — outcomes for key stakeholders. We're continually drawn to seeing what we do from the inside out.

The result of this bias is both serious and pervasive.

It's serious because it leads us to misread good performance on processes as competitive advantage. We think that by making them best practice or high quality we have automatically achieved competitive advantage. This notion is false but understandable when we recognise our shortsightedness in looking only from the inside out.

As we now know, competitive advantage is doing better on strategic factors in the eyes of our key stakeholders. *If* certain processes don't achieve this, they may not be important. *Unless* certain processes achieve this, they may best be abandoned. *Until* certain processes achieve this, they may not demand our attention.

As the keys to their success, many organizations list items described as "critical success factors" and "key result areas" (KRA's). These lists, and we've seen them time and time again in organizations and business units, are usually a confusion of internal processes, vague domains of activity, and perhaps a sprinkling of strategic factors. They're also not classified by key stakeholder.

Our problem as members of organizations and business units is that we become enmeshed in operations. We insist, and we can't help ourselves, on looking at our performance from an operations' point of view. Why? Because that is our preoccupation on a day-to-day basis. To be effective, however, we must take a strategic perspective. This is the outside-in view.

We look at our performance through their lens, not ours.

Once we take this view, we see ourselves as our key stakeholders see us. We adopt their criteria of assessment, not ours. We look at our performance through their lens, not ours.

We have now seen from this book that once you adopt this approach, you can develop strategy for a wide variety of organizations and business units. Profit-seeking organizations, of course, but also non-profit organizations in the public and private sectors can be approached in this way. Strategic factors also provide a common currency through which we can link our strategic planning — involving strategic analysis and strategy development — with performance measurement.

Chapters 2 to 11 have taken you through a series of steps that started with identifying key stakeholders and ended with writing a strategic action plan. The section below summarizes these steps, while the last section pulls together the benefits of the System outlined in this book.

1. Identify key stakeholders.

2. Identify strategic factors for key stakeholders.

3. Assess performance on strategic factors.

4. Set targets on objectives.

5. Develop strategy to achieve targets.

6. Set targets on strategic factors.

7. Write a strategic action plan.

We'd like to end this book by drawing you back to the results of employing strategic factors:

- *Connecting strategic analysis and strategy formulation*
  Connection clear and streamlined

- *Defining competitive advantage*
  Defined outside-in, not inside-out

- *Conducting competitive assessments and assessing*

competitive advantage
Focuses squarely on external factors

- *Establishing clear and quantified objectives*
Statements built around measurable outcomes

- *Writing clear and focused strategy*
Focused because the method is clear

- *Developing strategy for all key stakeholders*
Focus is on *all*

- *Developing strategy for non-profit organizations and for business units*
No difficulties, as the techniques can apply across all organizations and business units

- *Defining value*
Clarity of definition

- *Defining differentiation and positioning*
Linked and complementary

- *Developing strategy for lobbying, acquisitions, strategic alliances and innovation*
Clearly linked to competitive advantage

- *Relating strategy formulation and performance measurement*
Intimately linked

- *Developing key performance indicators*
Always strategy-driven

BENEFITS

What are the benefits clients achieve by following the approach outlined in this book? Which features of our System particularly help to improve the performance of their organizations and business units?

Below is a sample of their responses.

One feature clients nominate as a special benefit is that key stakeholders are identified *and* that they are linked throughout the entire process. This helps to think broadly about strategy, not simply to focus on customers or any other key stakeholders that happen to be pushed by vested interests within the organization or business unit. With a comprehensive view of the key stakeholders, the strategy development of our clients is more complete. They tell us also that in developing strategy this way, they can see the connections between key stakeholders, whereas previously, these connections were not clearly articulated.

Our clients also relate that a benefit of particular significance is the way in which objectives are set via behavioral outcomes. As we have said, this is a unique approach. It helps organizations and business units to cut through the usual platitudes that arise when objective setting is the task. Clients recount that by focusing on behaviors, they're better able to identify clear and measurable objectives. From these, they can then set precise targets. The benefit here is that by bringing together targets categorized by key stakeholders, they find it easier to debate not only the target levels themselves, but also the interaction between the targets.

A further area of significant benefit, we're informed, is the identification of strategic factors. Most clients are only partially aware of what these factors are and it's usually only for customers. In the past, they haven't thought, they say, of strategic factors for other key stakeholders such as employees and suppliers. They've traditionally taken the latter for granted.

Once strategic factors are clearly identified, sharp and focused strategy can be developed.

Clients reinforce the importance of starting with a clear list of key stakeholders, as this drives the identification of strategic factors. The benefits here are that sharp and focused strategy can be developed, based on strategic factors. The impact of strategy for one key stakeholder can be seen on strategy for others.

An additional and telling benefit is Strategy's Three S's. Clients find that in using the six options we've presented within these three strategy types for each of their key stakeholders and reviewing their applicability, no strategic option gets overlooked. They then go on to develop specific strategies within each option. This thorough and exhaustive approach to strategy making, our clients assure us, prevents pet projects and functional bias from driving strategy selection.

In the area of performance measurement, clients nominate the adoption of the key stakeholder's point of view as being of special significance. Like many organizations they are often overwhelmed by measures, mostly meaningless, based on activity, on being busy but not business-like, on operations but not strategy. By taking key stakeholders' perspectives on their performance, clients turn the measurement process around. They measure less but more effectively.

They do this, they say, by returning to strategic factors. It comes as a shock to many of them to realise that they do not understand the strategic factors appropriate to their key stakeholders, and, therefore, meaningful measurement is an impossibility. What they also realize is that many of their measures labeled "performance measures" have nothing to do

> **Once clients think of their performance from a stakeholder's point of view, they redefine performance itself.**

with performance. Once they think of their performance from a key stakeholder's point of view, they redefine performance itself.

Finally, clients *like* the System. We call it the Strategic Factor System since at its core lies what key stakeholders want from an organization or business unit.

By following the approach outlined in this book, you too will achieve the benefits described above.

You'll lift the performance of your organization *significantly*.

STRATEGIC VERSUS OPERATIONAL PLANS: IS THERE A DIFFERENCE AND DOES IT MATTER?

There is confusion in some organizations about the difference between strategic and operational plans. As a result, many business units within organizations complete strategic plans when they do not need to, or neglect to draw up a strategic plan when they should.

STRATEGIC VERSUS OPERATIONAL DECISIONS

A strategic decision is one that externally repositions an organization (or a business unit) in some way. That is, it changes the organization's competitiveness in its industry. For example, at the North Los Angeles region level of the Largesse Bank (not its real name, of course), a decision could be made to open or close a particular branch. Clearly, this is a strategic decision that will affect the region's performance in its industry.

An operational decision, in contrast, is one that takes as given the desired position in the industry and then develops the means by which that position can be achieved. (See Figure A.1.) For example, the Pasadena branch probably makes decisions on staff scheduling, office procedures and resource use within the branch, but probably does *not* make any strategic decisions. These have undoubtedly been taken at the North Los Angeles region level and other levels. The decision as to whether the branch will be closed is made by someone other than the Pasadena branch manager. Decisions regarding advertising, pricing, store presentation and customer service levels are also made by individuals outside the Pasadena branch. So, the branch manager is left with purely operational decisions.

Operational decisions are ones that pertain to efficiency rather than competitiveness (which is the province of strategic decisions) and are concerned with how to achieve designed outcome levels as inexpensively as possible.

STRATEGIC AND OPERATIONAL PLANS

In the organization chart of the Largesse Bank (Figure A.2),

Figure A.1 **Concepts and Guidelines**

Concepts	Definitions/Guidelines
• Strategic decision	• Focuses on competitiveness for an organization or business unit, e.g. customer service level, product range, price
• Operational decision	• Focuses on efficiency for an organization or business unit, e.g. allocation of staff, reporting relationships
• Strategic plan	• Is the embodiment of a set of strategic decisions, e.g. future direction of organization or business unit • Not to be done when an operational plan is all that is required • In large organisations needs to be undertaken also by support units, such as human resources, as they operate in an industry different from the organization of which they are a part. • Involvement in strategic planning and requiring a strategic plan for one's business unit are two different matters. • Must be truly "strategic," not re-labeled operational plans
• Operational plan	• Is the embodiment of a set of operational decisions, e.g. the production plan of a manufacturing organization • Should be undertaken by all business units in organizations (some of these business units will, in addition, have strategic plans)

we see that the bank is divided into three divisions, one of which, the Retail Banking Division, is divided into four regions; one of these, the North Los Angeles region, contains four branches. There would be a strategic plan at the corporate level, because the chief executive and others obviously make strategic decisions affecting the bank as a whole. There would be a strategic plan at the division level, since the divisional manager of Retail Banking and others make decisions that are strategic for the division. The North Los Angeles regional manager and others may also make strategic decisions and hence require a strategic plan. However, the Pasadena branch manager, whose decisions are operational, only requires an operational plan. The strategic decisions for the branch have been made at higher levels.

Figure A.2 **Largesse Bank**

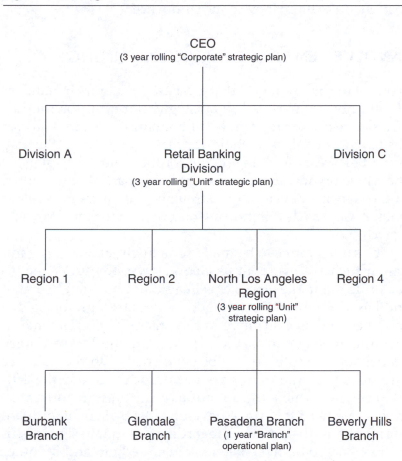

CEO
(3 year rolling "Corporate" strategic plan)

Division A

Retail Banking Division
(3 year rolling "Unit" strategic plan)

Division C

Region 1

Region 2

North Los Angeles Region
(3 year rolling "Unit" strategic plan)

Region 4

Burbank Branch

Glendale Branch

Pasadena Branch
(1 year "Branch" operational plan)

Beverly Hills Branch

The problem in many organizations is that this difference is not recognized. So, the manager of the Pasadena branch (or its equivalent) would be forced into developing a strategic plan and undertaking strategic analysis when it is totally unnecessary. And precisely because it is perceived as unnecessary, it serves to frustrate the individuals involved.

In addition to this frustration, the managers are diverted from their prime task, which is running the branch efficiently. They cannot understand why their attention is being deflected from the question of efficiency and focused, instead, on matters they cannot influence.

INVOLVEMENT IN STRATEGIC PLANNING

None of this is to suggest that the Pasadena branch manager should not be involved in strategic planning for the Los Angeles region or for the Retail Banking Division — or for the Largesse Bank as a whole, for that matter. He or she may be part of a team focusing on the corporate strategic plan for the whole organization. However, being part of one or more of those teams developing a strategic plan at those levels is not the same as developing a strategic plan for the Pasadena branch.

The same point can be made for a manufacturing organization such as Toyota. In its Georgetown, Kentucky manufacturing plant, the manager is in a similar position to that of the Pasadena branch manager — the strategic decisions have been taken elsewhere in the organization. The manufacturing manager in charge of producing the Toyota Camry model, for example, should be concerned with the quantity and quality of the motor vehicles produced and the efficiency with which the manufacturing system operates. There is no need for him to develop a strategic plan for manufacturing, as the decisions regarding pricing, design, distribution, and so on have been taken elsewhere and by other sectors of the organization.

Again, this does not preclude his being part of teams that make such decisions. However, his main job is to prepare an effective operational plan for efficient production of motor vehicles that meet standards.

SUPPORT UNITS WITHIN ORGANIZATIONS

From what we have said, it could be implied that support units such as human resources, finance, accounting and training do not require strategic plans. In most cases they don't, but in large organizations they do. Training, for example, is really a separate industry. The training department of the Largesse Bank applies its specialist knowledge and practices to the bank, but it remains part of the training industry. The Pasadena branch of the bank, in contrast, applies knowledge and practices that are peculiar to banking.

Because a support unit like training is part of a different industry, it faces a different set of competitors — other training suppliers. It should focus on them and develop a competitive advantage.

A support unit also needs to consider whether or not it should be outsourced, in whole or in part. Of course, this brings such a unit face to face with the question of competitiveness and, therefore, the need for a strategic plan.

CONCLUSION

A strategic plan embodies decisions regarding competitive advantage, future direction and scope of business activity; it increases the competitiveness of the organization or business unit concerned. Problems arise, and much time and resources are wasted, when complete strategic plans are required of individuals who should be focusing on operational plans. Problems also arise in large organizations when support units such as training, human resources and accounting are excluded from developing strategic plans and are left on the sidelines in the strategic planning process.

Involving a Board in Strategic Planning

There is considerable conjecture in board and management circles regarding the extent to which a board should be involved in strategic planning. Should it get into details or remain aloof from the process, letting management "get on with it," and only becoming involved at the final approval stage? Or is there an intermediate approach that captures the best elements of these two extremes?

The purpose of this appendix is to describe three options, weigh up the pros and cons of each, and recommend a generally desirable route for a board to take.

The material is based on several experiences that we have had in facilitating strategic planning sessions for organizations, but we especially draw on our observations of the lotteries organization we have written about in earlier chapters.

You will remember that this organization is government-owned and operates as a public sector corporation. Its products are lottery tickets, which are bought through retail stores acting as agents. As a public sector corporation, it pays an annual dividend to its owner, the government. Though a government corporation, it is run very much like a private sector organization, but it does have, as one would expect, some unusual reporting relationships to its owner, the government. Unlike a private sector organization, it is also subject to political influence.

The lotteries experimented with the two extremes outlined in this appendix. Let's now look at the first of these, which we call the "hands-on approach."

HANDS-ON APPROACH

In this approach, the board becomes intimately involved in the strategic planning activity. For example, board members, as well as the chief executive and members of the organization who make up the planning team, meet together as part of a strategic planning activity. The meeting may take place over two days at either a resort or city hotel. In this scenario, board members become "equal" partners with management in developing the strategic plan.

In the lotteries organization, board members sat down with a planning team composed of the CEO and sixteen other organization members. Over the course of two days, it developed the strategic plan with the CEO and his team.

A number of problems arose. For one thing, board members became too involved in the detail of the strategic plan and ended up actually trying to write the plan — despite their lack of sufficient in-depth industry knowledge to do it well.

Another problem was that the members of the planning team "sat back" and deferred to board members. They thought that the board members "had all the answers" and so were reluctant to speak up in their presence. Another reason for their reluctance was that the board members were not known to the team; they were, in effect, "strangers." Team members didn't feel right about talking plainly in front of them. Nor did they want to embarrass either the CEO or senior management by discussing problems of which the board might not be aware.

A further result of board members becoming too involved is that the plan may cease to be "owned" by the planning team itself. It may reflect what the board wants or what the planning team *thinks* the board wants, but it is no longer something for which the planning team and management feel accountable. Some may even describe the final product as the "board's plan."

For all these reasons, the "hands-on approach" as described here is generally to be avoided in strategic planning. It can be a real waste of the board's time and effort, since it does little, if anything, to improve the quality of either the planning process or the completed strategic plan.

HANDS-OFF APPROACH

Having experienced all the problems described in the previous section with no observable benefits from the "hands-on" approach, the lotteries board went to another extreme the next time the organization undertook its strategic planning.

In this "hands-off" approach, board members play little part in the strategic planning process until the plan has been fully developed. The strategic planning activity is undertaken by the chief executive and the planning team, whose members are drawn from within the organization. Typically, board involvement occurs when the chief executive presents the strategic plan to the board.

Unfortunately, the strategic plan the lotteries management produced recommended changes that did not meet board requirements. The result was that it was rejected by the board, and the strategic planning process was thrown into disarray.

One problem with the hands-off approach is that the planning team is in the dark regarding the board's expectations. As the latter are not expressed up front, the plan that is produced may well be one that the board does not like, as happened to the lotteries plan. When a board does not put in the time and effort to determine what its own requirements are, it is a case of trying to "shoot a moving target."

Another problem with the hands-off approach is the time that is wasted while the strategic plan is revised in the light of board expectations.

While a board's intentions may have been good, i.e. not to interfere, the hands-off approach does no one any good. Management has been forced to try to produce a plan that meets unknown criteria!

Clearly the two extremes, the "hands-on" and "hands-off approach," have their shortcomings. For this reason, we now turn to a third method.

PLANNING PARAMETERS APPROACH

In this approach, a board presents a set of planning parameters to its chief executive, who then takes them forward with his or her planning team. The parameters are broad guidelines for the development of the strategic plan. When the chief executive presents the team's plan to the board, it has the opportunity to assess it against the parameters it laid down at the beginning of the process.

An "elevator" is in operation here. (See Figure B.1.) The elevator starts with the board, moves down into the organization via the chief executive, to the planning team (or teams) and comes back up from the planning team (or teams) via the chief executive, to the board. The board starts the elevator moving by developing planning parameters that the chief executive and his or her planning team need to take into account in developing the strategic plan. At the end of the elevator's travel, the chief executive passes a strategic plan to the board that is in keeping with the board's own parameters.

Figure B.1   **Strategic Planning Process – Elevator Effect**

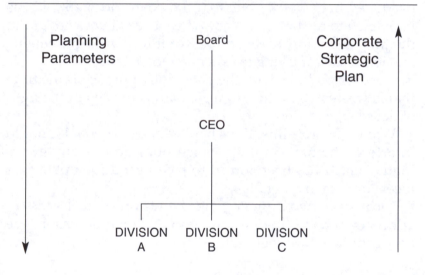

The lotteries organization, having had its previous experiences with board involvement, redesigned its planning to follow this parameters approach.

Among the benefits that followed was that the board members no longer wasted their time sitting in discussions that were often far too detailed for their participation. Further, planning team members were no longer placed in a position in which they felt a need to defer to board members. They had to make up their own minds as to what was best for the organization and what the details of the strategic plan should be. Management was no longer working in the dark, but within the planning parameters established by the board.

A further benefit from this approach is that it forces some discipline on a board: it can no longer sit back and wait for the strategic plan with the view that "we'd know a good one if we saw it." A board really has to sit down at the first stage of the planning process and decide what their assessment criteria (planning parameters) should be.

Under this approach, any changes that are required to the strategic plan, when it is presented to the board by the chief executive, are usually not radical. Planning is more stream-lined, too, since there is usually no need to backtrack.

EXAMPLES OF PLANNING PARAMETERS

Figure B.2 contains a number of examples of planning parameters that a board might employ or produce.

Figure B.2   **Examples of Planning Parameters**

Planning horizon for strategic plan (e.g. three years)

Capital expenditure limitations

Profit and cash flow in dollar terms

% return on shareholders' funds

% of revenue from exports

% of revenue from a certain product/service group

% of revenue from a geographic region (e.g. Asia)

% growth in revenue over planning period

Types of business the organization should embrace or avoid
(e.g., areas likely to involve litigation)

Policy on diversification and acquisition opportunities

Major impacts to be taken into account

The first one, the planning horizon, relates to the strategic plan itself. Some plans have a horizon of three years, others shorter and others longer. It depends on the industry and the amount of change occurring in it. For some industries, there is little certainty beyond a two-year span. Change is slower in others, and a longer period is not only possible, but highly desirable.

Another planning parameter that a board may devise relates to capital expenditure limitations. From its knowledge of the finances of the organization, a board may decide to restrict the amount of capital available to management. It may formulate this limitation on the basis of the organization's debt situation. Of course, it's important for a planning team to know this limitation up front, as it may restrict the activities proposed.

Other planning parameters relate to strategic plan outcomes such as profit, either in dollar terms or as a percentage of shareholders' funds, or as revenue, either by product group or geography or by domestic and export sources. A parameter that is clearly the province of a board is the required percentage return on shareholders' funds. As the representative of shareholders' interests, the board is in a position to lay down requirements to management in this regard. Naturally, these requirements would impact on profit and cash flow as well.

But a board may also rightly express a view on the sources of revenue. In Figure B.2, these streams are shown as a percentage of revenue from exports or certain product/service groups or geographic region. For instance, a CEO and his or her planning team may be told that certain revenues need to come from markets other than the domestic. A board may also provide guidelines to management regarding the percentage of revenue from new products as compared with older ones. It may suggest that certain geographic regions be avoided for social and political reasons, so as to take no risks.

Growth is another parameter to be considered by a board. A certain percentage return on shareholders' funds might be achieved at the expense of growth. So a board may require that revenue growth keep pace with the return on shareholders' funds.

The last three items in Figure B.2 relate to policy parameters. These might include the type of businesses the organization should avoid for reasons of litigation, for example, or a policy on diversification and acquisition.

Lastly, a board may identify certain major influences of an economic or social nature that need to be encompassed by the strategic plan.

These, then, are some of a variety of planning parameters that might be employed by a board.

CONCLUSION

In explaining these three distinct approaches, we have by no means exhausted the options available to a board for its participation in strategic planning. We have witnessed many others apart from these.

For various reasons, the hands-on and hands-off approaches have been found wanting, while the planning parameters approach has been found to have certain advantages. All boards and management should take a closer look at the strategic planning process that operates within their organizations. Boards should review the form their involvement takes and question whether or not that involvement compromises their ability to take an impartial view of the strategic plan once it is produced by management.

Boards should also consider whether they are giving sufficient guidance to management in their attempts to develop a satisfactory strategic plan. The requirement of boards to give guidance, yet be able to impartially assess a strategic plan that is developed by management, is generally met by the planning parameters approach.

COMPETITIVE ADVANTAGE ALONG VALUE CHAINS

In developing strategy, it is important to consider key stake-holders linked together in a value chain.

Value chains, which can be characterized as taking a raw material through to a finished product, exist in all industries. Manufacturing comes immediately to mind, but service industries also have value chains. In education, the uneducated become educated; in the hospital industry, ill people become well, and so on.

The value chain concept is an important one in developing strategy and competitive advantage for an organization or business unit. There are significant points in this chain at which we need to strive for competitive advantage and develop strategy. These points are clustered around certain key stakeholders.

VALUE CHAIN – FOR INDUSTRY OR ORGANIZATION?

Before proceeding, we have to consider the question: Is the value chain of our organization the value chain of our industry? The distinction is important.

The conventional way in which the term "value chain" is used is to describe activities within an organization. These activities include inbound logistics, operations, outbound logistics, marketing and sales, as well as support activities. But by describing a value chain this way, we restrict ourselves to those activities in which an organization is currently involved. They may be value-adding activities, of course, yet other sets of activities that could add additional value might be overlooked. In setting strategy and achieving competitive advantage, knowledge of these other activities is important to an organization's planning team.

For this reason, we use the term "value chain" in reference to the industry, not merely the organization. In Figure C.1, fruit-canning industry activities start with the raw materials, the fruit grown, and proceed to the finished product, canned fruit. This product then goes to the customer — in this case, large retailers — and moves from there to the consumer.

Figure C.1   **Value Chain, Fruit Canning Industry**

Raw ⟶ Finished ⟶ Customer ⟶ Consumer
materials   product

Industry Activities	Cannery Involvement
Growing fruit	Indirect
Picking fruit	Indirect
Transporting fruit	Direct
Processing fruit	Direct
Packaging fruit	Direct
Storing cans	Direct
Selling cans	Direct to large retailer
Distributing cans	Indirect to large retailer
Cans stored by large retailer (customer)	Nil
Cans sold by large retailer	Nil
Can contents consumed by purchaser (consumer)	Nil

The right-hand column of this Figure describes how one particular organization, a fruit canner, is involved in industry activities. Note that it is not involved in all of them, as indicated by the words "Indirect" and "Nil." Were we to describe the value chain as only those activities in which the cannery was involved, it would start with transporting fruit and finish with selling cans. The problem then would be that a planning team might not consider opportunities to capture additional value by taking in further activity, either upstream or downstream in the value chain.

VALUE CHAIN OR COST CHAIN?

Let's now consider the term "value." Is it really value or is it cost? Does the distinction matter?

We often delude ourselves into thinking that because we incur cost, we are thereby adding value. Yet we know that value is defined by key stakeholders, and key stakeholders are not interested in cost. They assess value on the basis of the strategic factors that apply to them.

Take customers and consumers, for instance. Which of the industry activities contribute to value for them? This is a difficult question. We're not sure. We are sure, however, that each of the industry activities incurs costs. So, to that extent, value chains are cost chains; some authorities describe them as such, rather than as value chains. Growing fruit, picking it, transporting it, processing it, packaging it all incur costs, as do storing cans, selling them, distributing them, and so on down the value chain.

So we know for certain that value chains are cost chains, and we have to look harder to determine whether they also add value.

Let's look at the industry activities from the point of view of the customer, the large retailer. The strategic factors relevant to the large retailer include the way in which the cans are delivered, the packaging of the cans in boxes, the trading terms between itself and the cannery. From this *customer's point of view*, then, the activities that impact on those strategic factors are packaging fruit and distributing cans. As the retailer doesn't consume the fruit, its quality — which is influenced by the industry activities of growing and picking, transporting and processing — is of little consequence.

A different perspective emerges when we consider industry activities from the *consumer's point of view*. What are the strategic factors here? Well, consumers *are* interested in the quality of the fruit. They're also interested in the labelling on the can, the price, and other strategic factors. So for them, the value-adding activities are those concerned with growing, picking, transporting, processing and packaging. As availability is also important to consumers, distribution is a value activity, too.

This way of looking at your industry value chains, through the eyes of your customers and consumers, is important for developing effective strategy. Industry activities take on a totally different perspective as compared to viewing them with the eyes of the organization or business unit.

It should be clear by now that what constitutes an industry value chain is not always clear! Sure, we can list the various activities that occur within an industry, but this list isn't the same as a value chain. We're looking for what adds value for our key stakeholders, especially customers and consumers. We know for certain that those activities add cost. We have to consider whether or not they add value.

Yet, we haven't replaced the term "value chain" by "cost chain" because strategy is vitally interested in the activities, as in Figure C.1, that add value for our customers and consumers.

COMPETITIVE ADVANTAGE ON A VALUE CHAIN

Think again about the cannery's involvement on the industry value chain, shown in Figure C.1. A technique you will want to try is to list the activities of *your* industry and your organization's involvement in them.

Detailing Involvement

The industry activities illustrated in Figure C.1 start with "growing fruit" and end with "can contents consumed by purchaser (consumer)." In between are "picking," "transporting," "processing," "packaging," "storing," "selling," "distributing cans," "storing and selling by the retailer."

This description of industry activities is, of course, a broad one. You need to keep it as broad as possible while still providing your planning team with sufficient detail to highlight your organization's involvement. But you can be very detailed in your description of an industry's activities.

You can also put down costs for each. For example, in the beef industry, the cost of a kilogram or pound of beef can be shown at every point in a detailed description of industry activities. However, it is usually not necessary for that level of detail to be placed in front of a planning team. In fact, it may only cloud the question of where our organization or business unit is involved in industry activities and what this tells us about our current and potential competitive advantage.

The mere listing of industry activities is a useful discipline in itself. Many individuals who have worked for your organization over several years and are part of your planning team don't have a clear picture of how value is added in your industry. This is because they have tended to concentrate on their own area of specialization, e.g., accounting, human resources, marketing or operations. While they know what they do in those areas and how they contribute to your organization, they have only a hazy idea of industry-wide activities and where your organization fits into these.

Hence the discipline of documenting industry activities via a value chain is an important and useful step in strategy development.

Competitive Advantage on Activities

The first thing we note from Figure C.1 is that the cannery is directly involved in a number of significant activities, a fact that gives rise to *potential* competitive advantage. Of course, being involved does not necessarily mean that competitive advantage has been achieved via superior performance on strategic factors. However, it does at least generate this opportunity.

The second thing to note is that, because the cannery is a cooperative, it is indirectly involved in two significant industry activities: growing and picking fruit. Its suppliers of fruit are the cannery's owners. This indirect involvement also delivers *potential* competitive advantage; compared to a competitor that buys its fruit on the open market, this cannery can control product quality, a strategic factor for consumers. If it can achieve superior quality, it will have a competitive advantage as far as consumers are concerned.

Blind Spots on Value Chains

The third thing to note is that the cannery has nil involvement at significant points in the value chain. This highlights the need to compensate for these potential "blind spots" through effective data gathering, which would involve monitoring how large retailers store and present the cans and doing market research to assess how consumers' tastes and preferences change.

But the cannery needs to be wary of the sources of its information. Its customer, the large retailer, can tell the cannery what sells but cannot tell it what it should make. To know that, the cannery must research its consumers; otherwise, it is likely to be led to produce what the large retailer can sell at ever lower prices.

In fact, this is exactly what has traditionally occurred in this industry. With most organizations production-oriented rather than marketing-oriented, the emphasis has been upon lowering costs to remain competitive. Innovation in packaging has not been a feature of the industry. It seems as though the canneries have relied too much on the information given to them by their customers, the large retailers, and have been followers rather than leaders of packaging change.

Developing Strategy

Detailing an organization's involvement in an industry value chain can also give rise to considerations of forward or backward integration. In the case of our cannery, the question might be asked whether competitive advantage would be enhanced if it took over the distribution of its cans instead of outsourcing. The strategy would be to improve delivery, which is one of the strategic factors relevant to large retailers.

Another consideration arising from a look at one's involvement in industry activities is the way in which the performance of *competitors* on strategic factors might be changed. In Chapter 9 we considered four of these ways: lobbying, strategic alliance, acquisition and innovation. Each of these Structure Strategy options can be employed along a value chain to alter industry structure, industry rules and competitor relationships and thereby improve competitive advantage.

Let's suppose that our cannery wished to change the performance of its competitors by acquiring one of the large contract distributors. It could then ensure that the contract distributor carried only the cannery's products, a policy that could restrict the ability of competitors to have their products distributed to certain large retailers.

Or the cannery could establish an alliance with a large retailing chain, for mutual benefit. This could effectively restrict the ability of competitors to obtain shelf space.

Another way in which the cannery could employ Structure Strategy is innovation. It could decide to turn the industry upside down by distributing peaches and pears, for instance, in glass bottles instead of cans. The glorious colours of the fruit would be on display rather than hidden in a can. This innovation could revolutionise the industry and make its competitors' technology obsolete.

Such straightforward examples of Structure Strategy show how knowledge of the value chain of an industry and an organization's involvement in it can be an effective tool to developing strategy and achieving competitive advantage.

Let's now turn our attention to two examples of organizations that have worked their industry's value chains and built their reputations along them.

SCANIA TRUCKS

Scania is a Swedish-owned manufacturer and distributor of trucks, buses, coaches and marine engines. The truck industry, like many others, is highly competitive, and just one-fifth are left of the makers within Europe that existed thirty-five years ago. Scania's customer base is becoming increasingly dominated by a few large fleet operators, such as the retailer Tesco, haulier Excel and the lease-and-rental company, Ryder. These purchasers exhibit considerable buying power.

Scania's trucks are generally regarded as premium products, and they command premium prices. Their major rival is Volvo, which has 20% of a static market. Scania is the only major player in the United Kingdom to have experienced a steadily increasing market share in the past decade. It intends to remain an independent organization and build organically. Its share of the UK market was 14% in 1994, and the aim is for more than 20% in the near future.

Scania's focus has moved from a product orientation (i.e. building trucks) to a broader definition of its business that encompasses wider transport solutions and customer service through the building of profitable partnerships along its industry's value chain — between Scania and its customers. Its mission statement now reads: "We are committed to providing optimum solutions to meet customer needs by building profitable partnerships driven by quality in all we do." This new statement reflects the changed emphasis.

Scania has reconfigured and extended its business. It has seen how value can be added through after-sales activity. One group of organizations within the value chain, the distributors, is now required to develop new value-adding services, which include contract hire and truck-leasing schemes, customized financial packages to help with truck purchase, emergency support services and off-site inspection and repair.

Interestingly, the most profitable side of the business, after-sales, which currently contributes over three-quarters of the network's profit, is being elevated in status compared with the higher-profile but lower-margin sales function.

Scania's experience illustrates the importance of comprehending the full value chain that exists in an industry and not simply the value activities an organization controls. By understanding the industry value chain, Scania is extending its influence to ensure that value is added from a customer's point of view. Customer input is sought via customer focus groups, and this input is used to generate improvements in the value-adding system. Scania thus hopes to increase its competitive advantage by improving customer service while maintaining its premium price position. It will work the value chain by emphasizing relevant strategic factors such as customer service, price and product quality.

LEVI STRAUSS

Levi Strauss is a privately held global corporation with headquarters in San Francisco, California. It produces jeans, jeans-related products and casual clothing in over 60 countries. Employing more than 36,000 people worldwide, it operates more than 76 production facilities that encompass cutting, pressing, finishing and other manufacturing activities.

Levi Strauss began operations in 1853 through the efforts of a Bavarian immigrant. In the 1980s the company expanded from its core blue jeans product and launched its Docker line of casual pants. This product line rapidly became one of the most successful new clothing products ever sold in the United States.

Levi Strauss recognizes that the strategic factor, company reputation, is its most valuable asset. It also recognises that a corporate reputation is global and that, if managed properly, it can become a competitive advantage. While its reputation is reinforced through the image that Levi Strauss projects in its advertising, the company sees reputation as more fundamental than image, deeper and more enduring, because it reaches into the "character" of an organization. It is embedded in and enhanced by the value chain in which it operates, extending from the suppliers of fabric through to the end consumer, the purchaser of the finished product.

All links in the chain are significant if Levi Strauss is to maintain and enhance its reputation. On the supplier side, it has over 600 contractors in more than 50 countries. Many of these are located in Third World countries, and Levi Strauss goes to great pains to ensure that standards are met in the areas of environment, ethics, health and safety, legal matters and responsible employment practices.

On the customer side (i.e. retailers), the company concentrates on raising its performance by focusing on strategic factors that include reducing lead times, providing accurate and on-time deliveries, ensuring product availability and replenishment. On the consumer side (i.e. the purchasers), Levi Strauss again seeks to raise its performance on strategic factors. One of these is product quality: the company strives to provide high quality garments.

The use of the value chain extends well beyond the organization's boundaries. It is not just a case of extracting higher profits from company-bound activities, but looking beyond these organizational boundaries to consider the value chain all the way from raw materials to finished product and on to the consumer. In doing so, Levi Strauss demonstrates the importance of the various linkages in a value chain: linkages between its contract suppliers and itself, between itself and its customers – the various retailers around the world – and between these retailers and Levi Strauss' consumers.

At each point where interfaces with key stakeholders are encountered, strategic factors must be focused on and competitive advantage achieved.

GLOSSARY

Listed here are the major terms employed in this book — which are also the ones that we use in our Strategic Factor System. We try to keep terms to a minimum. The definitions are our own and are based on the experience we have gained in working with planning teams in various organizations and industries.

Action plan A list of actions that need to be undertaken to implement strategy. An action plan states what is to be done, who is to do it and when it is to be completed.

Behavioral outcome A statement that describes what an organization or business unit wants a key stakeholder to do.

Competitive advantage The extent to which an organization or business unit delivers value superior to that of its competitors.

Differentiation How an organization or business unit distinguishes itself on strategic factors.

Diversification The extent to which the activities of an organization or business unit are spread across industries.

Industry The environment of an organization or business unit, composed of a set of customers, suppliers, competitors, etc.

Industry segment Part of an industry.

Intensification The extent to which the activities of an organization or business unit are focused on a few industries.

Key performance indicators (KPI's) Measures of performance that are central to success.

Key stakeholders Organizations, business units and people with whom an organization or business unit interacts and on whom it depends for success, e.g., customers, employees, owners, suppliers.

Key strategic issue An item that will have a significant impact on the prosperity of an organization or business unit and which must be addressed via the strategic plan.

Leading indicator A measure (indicator) that predicts results on another measure (indicator). Measures of strategic factors are leading indicators of measures of objectives.

Measure A metric such as number of units produced, percent market share or dollar revenue.

Mission A statement that expresses the fundamental purpose of an organization or business unit. It answers the question, "What business are we in?"

Objectives Statements that describe what an organization or business unit wants to achieve via its key stakeholders, e.g., to increase revenue from customers.

Operational plan A plan that takes as a given an organization's or business unit's competitiveness and develops the means by which this can be accomplished, e.g. marketing plan, manufacturing plan.

Outcome An end result for a key stakeholder, organization or business unit.

Positioning The placement of an organization or business unit in the minds of its key stakeholders based on strategic factors.

Scale Strategy A strategy type concerned with outperforming the competition on strategic factors in the present industry.

Scope Strategy A strategy type concerned with outperforming the competition on strategic factors in a different industry.

Strategic factors Criteria on which an organization or business unit has to do well in order to succeed; they are used by stakeholders to assess performance.

Strategic Factor System An integrated approach to identifying strategic factors, setting objectives and targets, writing strategy and actions, all classified by key stakeholder. Performance is monitored via a cause-and-effect model that links the above together.

Strategic plan A plan that achieves competitive advantage for an organization or business unit.

Strategy A statement that describes how competitive advantage is to be achieved on strategic factors.

Structure Strategy A strategy type concerned with changing competitors' performance on strategic factors.

Target A level of performance on a key performance indicator which an organization or business unit sets out to achieve.

Value What a key stakeholder gets for what it gives. It is based on a key stakeholder's assessment of results on its strategic factors.

Value chain A sequence of activities that illustrates how cost and hopefully value are built in an industry.

Values Beliefs about what is right or wrong, good or bad. Values of an organization or business unit guide its culture. Two examples would be respect for staff and technical excellence.

Vision A description of what an organization or business unit will be like in some years' time.

ANNOTATED BIBLIOGRAPHY

This list of references on strategy and performance measurement is by no means exhaustive. It contains those *books* that we have found relevant to this topic and *personal articles*. Apologies are given in advance for any omissions.

While there is no shortage of books and articles on strategy, there has been little advancement in either analytical or practical frameworks in the last decade — which is why we believe *Strategic Planning and Performance Management* is needed. Analytical techniques have been largely at a standstill and practical methods, say for developing strategy, have remained unaltered.

In contrast to the field of strategy, performance measurement has been a "hotbed" of developments in recent years; hence the more recent list below. These advances have particularly focused on practical methods for designing effective performance measures.

Andrews, K.R., *The Concept of Corporate Strategy*, Homewood: Irwin, 1987.
In its third edition in 1987, this book was first published in 1971. Provided the framework on which much of the Harvard Business School "business policy" texts were built.

Ansoff, H.I., *Corporate Strategy*, New York: McGraw Hill, 1965.
Widely recognized as the father of the field, Ansoff provided a framework and methods, many of which carry through to the present. Revised edition published in 1988 and still in print in 2004.

Argenti, J., *Practical Corporate Planning*, London: Routledge, 1989.
First published in 1980, this second edition seeks to provide a "simple system" based around SWOT (strengths, weaknesses, opportunities, threats) analysis. Regarded by many managers as "the bible" in its day.

Becker, B.E., Huselid, M.A. and Ulrich, D., *The HR Scorecard: Linking People, Strategy, and Performance*, Boston: Harvard Business School Press, 2001.

Built on the balanced scorecard model this book seeks to develop a HR scorecard to trace the contribution of the human resources function to organizational performance.

Camp, R.C., *Benchmarking: The Search for Industry Best Practices That Lead to Superior Performance*, Milwaukee: Quality Press, 1989.
The first book written on benchmarking and still one of the best. Written by the author while still "hot" from his experience at Xerox — relevant to performance measurement.

Deming, W.E., *Out of the Crisis*, Cambridge: Cambridge University Press, 1982.
Any book that touches on performance measurement must acknowledge the work of the quality movement and especially that of Deming. His fourteen points are as fresh as ever. If you'd like a more approachable book on the topic, as well as a book that places Deming in his historical context, read Gabor below.

Dunk, A.S. and Kenny, G.K., "Departmental Assessment: Managers' Perceptions of the Usefulness of Accounting and Non-Accounting Measures," *Canadian Journal of Administrative Sciences*, 1986, 3, 261-274.
Here we researched the usefulness of a set of measures to production and marketing managers. We were especially interested in the part that non-accounting measures played in departmental performance measurement. For further details see Kenny and Dunk below.

Freeman, R.E., *Strategic Management: A Stakeholder Approach*, Marshfield: Pitman, 1984.
Generally regarded as the book that formalized the introduction of "stakeholder" into strategic management.

Gabor, A., *The Man Who Discovered Quality*, New York: Penguin, 1990.
Read this book and understand the quality movement since the Second World War, as well as Deming's role in

the quality revolution. Entertaining, informative and relevant to performance measurement.

Hamel, G. and Prahalad, C.K., *Competing for the Future*, Boston: Harvard Business School Press, 1994.
A book read by many managers when first published. Interesting for its discussion of organizational core competencies as sources of competitive advantage.

Kaplan, R.S. and Norton, D.P., *The Balanced Scorecard: Translating Strategy into Action*, Boston: Harvard Business School Press, 1996.

Kaplan, R.S. and Norton, D.P., *The Strategy Focused Organization: How Balanced Scorecard Companies Thrive in the New Business Environment*, Boston: Harvard Business School Press, 2001.
Our approach to performance measurement differs from theirs. Their method uses four pre-set categories called "perspectives": financial, customer, internal business process, and innovation and learning. Of course our system for objective setting, identifying strategic factors, developing leading indicators, etc, is absent from their techniques. The major contribution of both books is that they've given legitimacy to the use of non-financial measures at senior management levels.

Kenny, G.K. and Dunk, A.S., "Evaluative Differences for Production and Marketing Subunits: Australian Managers' Perceptions," *Asia Pacific Journal of Management*, 1986, 3, 99-109.

Kenny, G.K. and Dunk, A.S., "Performance Criteria for Production Subunits in Australian Manufacture," *Asia Pacific Journal of Management*, 1988, 5, 225-230.

Kenny, G.K. and Dunk, A.S., "The Utility of Performance Measures: Production Managers' Perceptions," *IEEE Transactions on Engineering Management*, 1989, 36, 47-50.
Was this research ahead of its time? Another interpreta-

tion is that in academia rewards flow from generating publications, not from applying ideas. Either way, this research laid the foundations for some of the concepts in this book as it investigated the usefulness of measures to production and marketing managers and the underlying drivers of measure utility. (See also Dunk and Kenny above.)

Kenny, G.K., "Taking a New Look at Competitive Advantage," *Company Director*, 2001, November, 15-17.
Points out the importance of distinguishing strategic factors from internal processes and capabilities and how this distinction has a major impact on the way strategy is developed.

Kenny, G.K., "Strategic Planning and Directors, Liability," *Company Director*, 2002, December, 17-20.
Explains the fundamental importance of having a strategic plan that is best practice and fully implemented. The article proposes that if this isn't the case company directors may be legally liable for consequent losses, including losses from missed opportunities. It also provides guidelines to achieve best practice.

Kenny, G.K., "Balanced Scorecard: Why It Isn't Working," *Management*, 2003, March, 32-34.
An article that has created much interest because of the current pervasiveness of the Balanced Scorecard. It analyses its failings as a method and suggests a different approach which avoids the traps that the Balanced Scorecard has fallen into.

Kenny, G.K., "Strategy Burnout," *Management*, 2003, August, 43-45.
Observes that "strategy" is becoming overused, misused and misunderstood. The article suggests a way to define competitive strategy that avoids confusing it with "operations". It draws on examples to illustrate the pitfalls of such confusion.

Kenny, G.K., "Growth Strategies: What and How to Choose," *Management*, 2003, December, 95-97.
Reviews the growth options open to companies, such as cloning and acquisition, and evaluates the advantages and disadvantages of each. But first the article discusses the question: Is growth for your organization?

Kenny, G.K., "Commodity-Price Trap," *Marketing*, 2004, March, 24-26.
Reviews how customers see certain products and services as commodities. The article explains why this occurs and provides a number of specific actions businesses can take to avoid this occurring.

Mintzberg, H., *The Rise and Fall of Strategic Planning*, Hemel Hempstead: Prentice Hall, 1994.
An interesting book by a prominent academic that from our experience has had negligible impact on either strategic planning's acceptance or practice — partly because it is based on a dated model of strategic planning. Ansoff's reply was: "My overall response to Henry's paper [based on the book] is that his understanding of planning was frozen in 1964."

Neely, A., Adams, C. and Kennerley, D., *The Performance Prism*, London: Prentice Hall, 2002.
This book was published after the first edition of this volume (2001) and presents, coincidentally, a framework with some similarities to our own – such as, the emphasis on stakeholders as the organizing principle in performance measurement and the view that measuring performance is concerned with measuring both sides of a relationship.

Porter, M.E., *Competitive Strategy: Techniques for Analyzing Industries and Competitors*, New York: The Free Press, 1980 and republished with new introduction in 1998.

Porter, M.E., *Competitive Advantage: Creating and Sustaining Superior Performance*, The Free Press, 1985 and republished with new introduction in 1998.

Porter, M.E., *The Competitive Advantage of Nations*, The Free Press, 1990 and republished with new introduction in 1998. These are landmarks that provided a quantum leap forward in the field of strategy and have remained continuously in print. We see ourselves as providing additional substance to his first two books. For example, to us his "generic strategies" — "low cost" and "differentiation" — are points on a continuum defined by strategic factors.

Ries, A. and Trout, J., *Positioning: The Battle for Your Mind*, New York: McGraw-Hill, 1981.
A classic revised in 1987 and still in print. Full of examples of firms that get marketing and positioning right and wrong.

Steiner, G.A., *Strategic Planning: What Every Manager Must Know*, New York: The Free Press, 1979.
The remarkable thing about some strategic planning books is their longevity — see Ansoff's book above and Steiner's here. This book is still in print in its original form, although its techniques look dated now.

Treacy, M. and Wiersema, F., *The Discipline of Market Leaders*, London: Harper Collins, 1995.
An interesting book in which the authors posited that there were three "value disciplines" — operational excellence, product leadership, and customer intimacy. Especially focused on customers of business organizations.

Zairi, M., *Measuring Performance for Business Results*, London: Chapman & Hall, 1994.
More on performance measurement from a "quality" perspective. Contains some interesting examples of measures employed by different businesses.

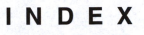

INDEX